the Body Snatcher

Boris Karloff as John Gray in *The Body Snatcher* (1945).

Cold-Blooded Murder, Robert Louis Stevenson and the Making of a Horror Film Classic

by
Scott Allen Nollen
with Yuyun Yuningsih Nollen

Foreword by Gregory William Mank

BearManor Media
2021

The Body Snatcher: Cold-Blooded Murder, Robert Louis Stevenson and the Making of a Horror Film Classic

© 2021 by Scott Allen Nollen
with Yuyun Yuningsih Nollen

All rights reserved.

No portion of this publication may be reproduced, stored, and/or copied electronically (except for academic use as a source), nor transmitted in any form or by any means without the prior written permission of the publisher and/or author.

Published in the United States of America by:

BearManor Media

BearManor Media
1317 Edgewater Dr #110
Orlando FL 32804

bearmanormedia.com

Printed in the United States.

Typesetting and layout by John Teehan

Cover photo: *The Body Snatcher* (1945) Boris Karloff, Russell Wade, Rita Corday and Sharyn Moffett (six-sheet poster).

Back cover photo: *The Body Snatcher* (1945) Boris Karloff (insert poster).

ISBN—978-1-62933-694-7

for
Donald Craig ["Blowzer"] Nance

Sing me a song of a lad that is gone,
Say, could that lad be I?
Merry of soul he sailed on a day
Over the sea to Skye.

Table of Contents

Preface: Trailing Tusitala ix

Foreword by Gregory William Mank 1

1 The Iniquitous Exploits of Burke and Hare 7

2 Young Robert Louis Stevenson and
   "The Body-Snatcher" 19

3 *The Body Snatcher*: The Val Lewton Production 53

4 Exploiting *The Body Snatcher* 83

5 Dissecting *The Body Snatcher* 105

6 Resurrecting R.L.S. 199

   Notes 215

   Bibliography and Sources 221

   About the Authors 225

   Index 227

Preface

Trailing Tusitala

I HAVE SEEN *THE BODY SNATCHER* (1945) more often than any other film. After the 100th time, I stopped counting, and that was two decades ago. I also have written about it more than any other film, comprising a chapter in my 1994 book *Robert Louis Stevenson: Life, Literature and the Silver Screen* and sections of my three volumes on Boris Karloff, published between 1991 and 2021. A few years back, I petitioned the Library of Congress to nominate it for inclusion in the National Film Registry, a valiant but vain attempt.

The first Stevenson story I heard was *Treasure Island*. While still a *bairn*, I listened with rapt attention as my father read the novel to me during a succession of bedtime story nights. My initial experience of reading Stevenson's work, after discovering a well-worn paperback of collected stories among the family books, occurred at about age nine. Prior to tackling *The Strange Case of Dr. Jekyll and Mr. Hyde*, I thought that "The Body-Snatcher," a short story, made more sense as an introduction. And, as much as I was intrigued by the more familiar title of the famous novella, the graverobbing designation proved irresistible to a lad who was mesmerized by Boris Karloff films such as *Frankenstein* and *The Mummy*, which, on a rare Saturday evening, would air on local commercial television.

In 1972, free from technological distractions, including video (which wouldn't arrive in my domain for six more years), reading was still the alpha and omega of entertainment, and, dare I say, enlightenment. Right and proper, Stevenson's story came first, since I was unable to see the film adaptation until after receiving a videocassette copy (containing a very dark, inferior television print) at Yuletide 1980.

Until I met my wife and literary partner in crime, YuyunYuningsih Nollen, in 2017, three of the greatest loves of my life were Scotland, Robert Louis Stevenson and Boris Karloff. Combined, they are an all-consuming passion. At the time *Robert Louis Stevenson: Life, Literature and the Silver Screen* was taking shape, my dream was to, one day, travel to Samoa, where I would visit "Tusitala's" home, Vailima, and tomb atop Mount Vaea, where he is interred beside his wife, Fanny Osbourne Stevenson.

Though I never made it to Samoa, I ended up more "far and away" than that, on the South Seas island of Java, in Indonesia. After I became permanently disabled and seriously ill in 2010, I thought my days of being "The Vagabond Scholar" were over; but little did I know that I would subsequently make a Herculean struggle, traveling more than 100,000 miles between the Western and Eastern hemispheres to get married, therefore prolonging my existence and surviving to write several more books, including this one. Like my literary hero, inspiration and posthumous mentor, I am now in the South Seas, writing with evermore devotion, about Scotland. If it wasn't true, this would read like a Hollywood movie, which brings us to the central subject of this book.

Though I was born in the States, I am indeed a *Scott*. The research and writing of *Robert Louis Stevenson: Life, Literature and the Silver Screen* began in 1989, and was greatly inspired by a journey to Scotland in September and October 1990. While enjoying the infinite attractions of Auld Caledonia, I investigated and located many actual sites used by Stevenson in some of his most famous stories, including his superb novel *Kidnapped* (1886).

To absorb the atmosphere of "The Body-Snatcher" (written in 1881) on a first-hand basis, I trekked through the Pentland Hills, a picturesque range of braes southwest of Edinburgh, into Midlothian, to explore the kirkyards of Glencorse and Penicuik, where the Fishers Tryst pub was still providing refreshments for the local inhabitants and at least this one visitor. "That's *no* the stuff they import to the States, Yank," one of them announced.

In those pre-internet days, I benefited from the assistance of the kindly Mrs. P. Ciupik, keeper of a bed-and-breakfast at Polton Bank, Edinburgh, whose German Shepherd, "Kate," was more than willing to wolf down the signature Scottish sausages that kept adorning my breakfast plate. Asked about the composition of said sausages, Mrs. Ciupik replied, "Well, lad: beef, pork and a wee bit o' sheep, *tae* be sure." Even if it seemed mostly (in Stateside vernacular) "mystery meat" to me, the high protein served me well during the daylong exploration of the locales used by Stevenson in his story geared to frighten the *Very De'il Himsel'*.

While in Penicuik, some real "snatching" did occur, when an attendant at a filling station purloined the petrol cap from the rental car after he had "topped it off." This necessitated plugging the intake of the tank over the weekend, until a new cap could be purchased the following Monday, at an auto parts store near Glasgow, about 55 miles to the northwest.

During my wanderings, I experienced many other Scottish locales that figure into the story of this book, related not only to Stevenson's story but also the historical events that inspired it. Prominent sites in the exploits of Burke and Hare included Greyfriars Kirk and the anatomical laboratory of Dr. Robert Knox.

Several Scottish historians and Stevenson scholars contributed to *Life, Literature and the Silver Screen*, for which they offered many kind words after its publication. My friend, the late Dr. Ernest Mehew, of Stanmore, Middlesex, was an independent scholar with many connections to British institutions of higher learning, notably the National Library of Scotland. His investigative quest involving a rare original Stevenson letter in my possession at the time (RLS was notorious for leaving his missives undated), in which he was assisted by Robin A. Hill of Edinburgh, resulted in not only an accurate date but also important details that informed that book and, nearly 30 years later, this one.

The letter, included in the 1994 book, subsequently was published in Mehew's multi-volume, Yale University edition of Stevenson's letters and now resides in the permanent collection of Stevenson manuscripts at the Silverado Museum in St. Helena, California. The location of Stevenson's honeymoon, it provided an unforgettable memory after I was asked to speak at the museum by the former curator, the late Edmond

Reynolds, who, along with the large gathering there, greatly appreciated the book. (The letter also is reproduced in chapter two here.)

The speaking engagement at Silverado led to an invitation from the Earl of Moray to visit his ancestral Caledonian domain, which includes the actual location of Stevenson's 1880 short story "The Pavilion on the Links," near North Berwick, a small town northeast of Edinburgh on the Firth of Forth. Unfortunately, I was forced by a circumstance beyond my control to turn down this beneficent offer, which would have provided benefits untold for a Stevenson aficionado. *Woe betide this lad for forsaking the Bonnie Earl o' Moray!*

The origins of this book on *The Body Snatcher* stretch all the way back to 1980, however; and the actual writing began 35 years ago, while I was attending an excellent class on the classic horror film, taught by the late Dr. Edward Lowry, a professor from Southern Methodist University in Dallas, Texas. In 1985, he was visiting my alma mater, the University of Iowa, for one semester. The final test for the course, as assigned by Lowry, standing in front of the theater screen in the university's Communication Studies building, decked out in his requisite blue jeans and cowboy boots, was to submit an original, forensic-level analysis of a single, formidable scene in a vintage fright film.

For me, there were only two choices: either the "creation scene" achieved by director James Whale, cinematographer John J. Mescall, and editor Ted J. Kent in *Bride of Frankenstein* (1935) or the hair-raising climactic sequence in *The Body Snatcher*. Since I was a lifelong admirer of Stevenson, and already had probed the adapted scene many times (during daydreams *and* nightmares), the process involved preparing a detailed storyboard-like chart of the scene (while relying on the decidedly imperfect "freeze frame" on my old Sony Betamax machine, while watching a dark, contrast-bereft print). The gambit payed off: In the words of Professor Lowry, written across the top of my paper, "This was an inspired choice..."

Lowry and I had planned to write what became *Boris Karloff: A Critical Account of His Screen, Stage, Television, Radio and Recording Work* as a collaborative effort, but his untimely death later that year (at age 34) rattled me to my foundations and forced me to forge ahead on my own. Dedicated in part to his memory, the book was published in 1991.

Creating *Robert Louis Stevenson: Life, Literature and the Silver Screen* necessitated reading the prolific author's entire output of novels, short stories, poetry, essays and travel books (even the many works left unfinished at the time of his death at age 44 in 1894). This exploit, achieved "old school" by checking out the hardcover library tomes and toting them around for endless months, also insured that Stevenson would evermore serve as my posthumous literary mentor. To reference Russell Wade's "Donald Fettes" in *The Body Snatcher*: I benefited from fine English and literature instructors during my pre-collegiate days, but that experience provided only the mechanics of writing. The poetry in crafting prose came from an outstanding professor during a graduate seminar in U.S. foreign policy, and from the Scots-suffused stories and verse of Robert Louis Balfour Stevenson.

After the book was published in 1994, misinformation continued to creep into general writings on *The Body Snatcher*; not necessarily about the film adaptation but concerning the Burke and Hare case or Stevenson's career. Over the past quarter-century, much additional research has been undertaken to provide the expanded coverage herein. As a "historian who writes about films," I also provide some context for the period in which *The Body Snatcher* was written and produced, when the world was neck-deep in an abominable global war. Ironically, in Tinsel Town, while millions were being massacred in real life, the producer, Val Lewton, would face hurdles from a major arbiter of public morality, accusing him of promulgating "excessive gruesomeness" in the realm of the "reel."

Stevenson suffered mightily all his short life from major illnesses and was forced continually to seek more amiable climes in the hope of improving his miserable physical condition. He spent most of his writing time in bed, and his maladies encompassed both bronchial and gastric problems. As much as I admire him, the thought of *becoming* like him, beyond learning a wee bit from his literary prowess, never entered my mind. But, physically laid low by side effects from treatment for a previous life-threatening illness, I permanently lost the ability to stand and walk, as well as developing a near-fatal infection from salmonella poisoning, the effects of which also are incurable.

Beginning to muster enough strength to write in various hospital beds, I was able to complete several new books, and thereafter had to do my research and writing while sitting in bed or the relative comfort of a sofa or overstuffed chair. In fact, at one point, I was informed by a physician that I had "only 12 to 24 hours to live." Fortunately, his diagnosis proved incorrect.

In his excellent 2018 book *The Scenery of Dreams: The True Story of Robert Louis Stevenson's "Kidnapped,"* Lachlan Munro writes,

> Stevenson's health was never so bad as during his three years in Bournemouth, and he frequently was in imminent danger of death from pulmonary haemorrhages, compounded by periods of blindness. Mostly confined to bed, he was forbidden to speak for weeks on end, and he was obliged to communicate by signs and notes… However, it was under these extraordinary conditions that he did most of his best work; like some latter-day Scheherazade, *telling tales to stay alive* [my emphasis]—*The Strange Case of Dr. Jekyll and Mr. Hyde, Kidnapped,* "Olalla" and "Markheim." He finished *Prince Otto, The Dynamiter* and *A Child's Garden of Verses*. A frequent visitor was the American writer, Henry James, who believed that Stevenson worked better when confined to his bed—the illness made his mind more active, and the seclusion helped him, defending from all interruptions—when he was well he played and talked, when he was ill he wrote. His life-threatening illness turned out to be the greatest facilitator of his imaginative genius, as it had been in childhood.[1]

As far as literary ability is concerned, no one else is Stevenson; and I have no equivalent of Henry James, although my constant companion, Yuyun Yuningsih Nollen, also is my greatest inspiration. When Stevenson was too ill to write, he dictated, often to his stepdaughter, Isobel. When he couldn't speak, he used sign language. I can do neither. Yuyun is an outstanding researcher and writes in her native language (which we then translate); but, so far, I don't require an amanuensis.

As "fate" would have it, I abandoned a northern land often beset by ice and snow for a sub-equatorial region of tropical heat and humidity; but I bypassed Samoa and reached Java, to roll in the footsteps of "Tusitala" (the name Samoan chiefs bestowed on Stevenson after he learned their language and intervened diplomatically in local political affairs). Like RLS, domiciled with his wife and stepson at Apia, where he created some of his finest writing, I practice a reasonable facsimile with mine at Bandung.

In developing *The Body Snatcher*, Val Lewton did a remarkable job of transferring the world of Stevenson's short story into a low-budget cinematic milieu, created entirely in Southern California. Stevenson not only knew about the locales he describes in his story, he *lived* in them. In retaining these actual sites for his screenplay, Lewton depicted them so convincingly that a viewer may believe that the producer-writer had paid them a visit. More than a century after Stevenson had walked the many miles through Edinburgh, the Pentland Hills and Midlothian, I fortunately had a similar experience. Writing this book brings enormous satisfaction. Yuyun Yuningsih Nollen and I hope

The Stevenson family at Vailima: Lloyd Osbourne, Margaret Stevenson, Isobel Strong, Robert Louis Stevenson, Austin Strong, Fanny Stevenson and Joe Strong, Apia, Upolu, Samoa, 1892.

The Nollen family at Manglayang: Yuyun Yuningsih Nollen, Scott Allen Nollen and Julio, Bandung, West Java, Indonesia, 2020.

that it will stand as a worthy companion to this outstanding motion picture.

We owe particular thanks to Gregory William Mank, a fine film historian and fellow Karloff (and Lugosi) scholar, whose early literary works helped inspire my own four decades ago. It is a privilege to include his deeply considered and entirely relevant thoughts on *The Body Snatcher* as the foreword to our own text. Always a pleasure to be in solidarity with "so learned a man." (All of us who hold *The Body Snatcher* in high esteem have benefited from his research in those RKO records now held hostage by a corporate culture that has adversely affected and even curtailed many similar efforts of scholarship, including some of my own.)

A special acknowledgment goes to my lifelong friend, Ontario geologist and film-memorabilia collector extraordinaire Kris Marentette, who kindly supplied many of the illustrations scanned from original *Body Snatcher* publicity materials, including the lobby cards and most of the still photographs. I also would like to mention (for their interest, assistance and contributions during the past three decades) the following individuals, who either reside in this world or, alas, beyond: Seamus Carney, Roy Gullane, Lachlan ["Lachie"] Munro, David Pegg, Gary Don Rhodes, Andy M. Stewart and Peter G. Vasey of the Scottish Record Office, Edinburgh.

Finally, Yuyun and I assume readers of this book already have seen *The Body Snatcher* prior to reading this book, especially chapter five ("Dissecting *The Body Snatcher*"). On the extremely unlikely chance that someone has *not* (and are averse to "spoilers," a term that didn't exist when I began watching, studying and writing about films more than a half-century ago; and certainly is impractical in any formal analysis of cinema), it is your responsibility to have the unforgettable experience of watching it first. (After all, I have seen the film more than 100 times, and I enjoy it more *every* time.) Definitely complete your own observation of the subject prior to perusing the post mortem!

– Scott Allen Nollen
At the foot of Manglayang Mountain,
Cileunyi, Bandung, West Java

Foreword
by Gregory William Mank

NEVER GET RID OF ME, Never Get Rid of Me, Never Get Rid of Me....

The Body Snatcher is the greatest horror film of the 1940s.

It's also my favorite horror film of the 1940s—and one of my favorite films, period.

The film's macabre blessings are abundant:

- Boris Karloff hauntingly portrays smiling, singing, graverobbing, murdering and ultimately spectral Cabman John Gray, in what is arguably his greatest all-time performance.

- Val Lewton, the film's producer, masterfully mixes his flair for atmospherics with blood-and-thunder melodramatics, his film based on Robert Louis Stevenson's 1881 tale about the historic "resurrection men" Burke and Hare.

- Robert Wise, the director, destined for Academy Awards for *West Side Story* and *The Sound of Music*, brilliantly brings depth to the story, making it a moving tragedy.

- Henry Daniell, as the proud, tormented Dr. "Toddy" MacFarlane, is superb.

- Bela Lugosi, as dense, doomed janitor Joseph, transcends a featured role added for box office hype, showing what a versatile actor he truly could be.

- All facets of the film deliver: Robert De Grasse's moody cinematography; Roy Webb's dramatic and at times beautiful musical score; the chilling use of sound (for example, the clop-clopping of Karloff's horse on the cobbled streets, which eventually becomes a terrifying harbinger of horror-to-come), and Philip MacDonald's literate screenplay, much of it revised by Lewton himself.

- There's even a memorable animal performance: "Little Robbie," the dog who faithfully guards his dead master's grave—and who falls victim to the Body Snatcher.

And, of course...
Never Get Rid of Me, Never Get Rid of Me...
There's the rip-roaring, spine-tingling climax, Gray seemingly having risen from the grave (yet still a corpse), riding on a coach on a stormy night, apparently naked, his ghastly white arm draped around the terrified MacFarlane—all preceded by Karloff's taunting "Never Get Rid of Me" refrain, hissing through the rain and the wind.

Karloff's Gray has become a "resurrection man," indeed.

My high regard for the film has deepened over the decades, due to personal experiences which have made me feel strangely close to it. Some examples:

When I was 25 years old and determined to learn as much as possible about my favorite films, I wrote to Robert Wise, asking if he'd send me a few memories of *The Body Snatcher*. Wise at the time was one of Hollywood's most prominent and immensely successful filmmakers, and I actually didn't expect a reply. Yet one day in the mailbox was a long, wonderful letter from Wise, packed with memories of Lewton, Karloff, Lugosi, the budget, the production and so on. Wise was sure to let me know that the film was also one of his personal favorites.

About seven years later, on a research trip to Hollywood, I visited the RKO Archives based in a warehouse in the Korean neighborhood near Hollywood. RKO had been out of business for over 25 years and this warehouse contained the studio's corporate history. There, the curator provided me with saddlebags of letters, contracts, and all the paperwork nuts-and bolts regarding the production of *The Body Snatcher*. When I noted there seemed to be little on Karloff in the saddlebags, the curator said, "Oh, he has his *own* file," and another saddlebag came to my table.

(Much of this material is now under lock-and-key at the Turner empire in Atlanta, Georgia. Researchers are turned away. I was lucky to review it when I did.)

I talked with members of the cast, as well as Lewton's widow and son. My dad had an Army buddy who, before they went overseas in World War II, was stationed with him in California; the buddy had visited the set of *The Body Snatcher* and had a funny Karloff story. I could go on, but suffice to say that, during my visits to the Monster Bash Convention in Mars, Pennsylvania, the past few years, Sharyn Moffett—who gave such a lovely performance as the crippled little girl Georgina in *The Body Snatcher*—has had a table right across from mine.

At times, it almost feels that I was somehow part of the movie. It's a nice sensation.

This is one of those films which has a double dose of theatrics—those in the film, and those in the production. This was, for example, the eighth and final film teaming of Karloff and Lugosi. Their big scene, where Karloff "burkes" Lugosi, is superb—all the more so because of the sensitive personal and professional situation that existed between the two men.

It was also a special film for Val Lewton's "Snake Pit" unit. This was RKO's challenge to Universal's "Monster rally" *House of Frankenstein*, which had also starred Karloff as a Mad Doctor resurrecting the Wolf Man (Lon Chaney), Dracula (John Carradine) and Frankenstein's Monster (Glenn Strange). Two very different types of Hollywood horror, battling it out for box-office supremacy.

And it was a production in which the vital prime movers—Lewton, Wise, Karloff, Daniell, Lugosi and really the entire company—were trying to rise far above the hokum to which Hollywood Horror had sadly descended.

They succeeded spectacularly.

The film was made with respect, and genuinely, love. One of my favorite stories about the shoot:

Thursday night, November 9, 1944: *The Body Snatcher* company was working on the RKO ranch in the San Fernando Valley. They were on the old set of *The Hunchback of Notre Dame* (1939); once medieval Paris, the set this night was playing 1831 Edinburgh.

The scene: Gray's murder of the lovely Street Singer, to get a cadaver to sell to MacFarlane without the danger of robbing an actual grave.

The audience will see and hear the Street Singer, her soprano voice rising in the night, moving away from the camera, into darkness. Then they see the Body Snatcher's carriage, his horse's hoofs clopping on the cobbled street. The horse, coach and driver follow the Street Singer into the blackness—and suddenly, in the midst of a high note, she stops singing.

Playing the Street Singer was Donna Lee. Playing the Body Snatcher, of course, was Boris Karloff. As Robert De Grasse prepared to shoot the scene, there was no real need for Karloff to be there. All that would be seen of the Body Snatcher, from the back, was his top hat. A double, stand-in, or stunt man could easily have taken over for Karloff. Actually, considering the angle, an RKO starlet in a bathing suit and wearing Karloff's top hat could have been riding the coach.

Karloff, of course, wouldn't hear of a double. There he was, despite the late hour, the cold, the major back surgery he recently had had, riding the coach.

The Street Singer disappeared into what the script called "Stygian darkness." The coach followed. Her singing stopped.

"Cut!" cried Robert Wise. Donna Lee was dismissed at 9:50 P.M. Karloff stayed on, dismissed at 10:45 P.M. from the "Edinburgh" location, arriving back at RKO at 11:30 P.M., then heading home to Coldwater Canyon at midnight.

He was having the time of his life.

* * *

Last year, my wife Barbara and I visited Edinburgh. The real-life history of the locale is fascinating, but I must admit that as I walked the streets, visited the castle, and saw the ancient graveyards, I imagined I was amidst the haunts of Karloff's Body Snatcher, Henry Daniell's MacFarlane, and Bela Lugosi's Joseph.

The Body Snatcher is about bodies, of course, but primarily it's about souls. This film glistens with the depth of the characters it presents, and the brilliance of the talent who unforgettably created it.

It's an honor to write this Foreword to Scott Allen Nollen's book about this remarkable movie.

– Gregory William Mank
March 2020

(Gregory William Mank is the author of such books as It's Alive! The Classic Cinema Saga of Frankenstein; Lugosi and Karloff: The Expanded Story of a Haunting Collaboration; *and* Laird Cregar: A Hollywood Tragedy. *He has also provided audio commentaries for various classic horror films and appears in the Blu-ray release of* The Body Snatcher *in the documentary,* You'll Never Get Rid of Me: Resurrecting The Body Snatcher.*)*

1

The Iniquitous Exploits of Burke and Hare

IN THE EARLY 1800S, Edinburgh, Scotland, was a major center for the study of anatomy, rivalling Leiden, Netherlands, and Padua, Italy. Edinburgh's reputation was assured by such doctor-instructors as Alexander Monro, John Bell, John Goodsir and Robert Knox. Required by Scottish law, medical researchers were allowed only to use the corpses of deceased prisoners, suicide victims, foundlings and orphans. At a time when high demand coincided with a shortage of legally available corpses, body snatchers, or "resurrection men," began to contribute "unfairly" obtained subjects to the supply delivered to anatomists. Though stealing a body was not a crime, as it had no owner, disturbing a grave and the taking of property from a deceased person were considered criminal offenses.

By the 1820s, Edinburgh residents began to take measures against the possible disinterring of their departed loved ones, including hiring guards and constructing watchtowers in cemeteries, and placing temporary stone slabs or iron cages, known as "mortsafes," over graves. These precautions greatly deterred graverobbing, resulting in a troubling shortage for the city's anatomists.

By the mid-19th century, the names of William Burke and William Hare became synonymous with the act of graverobbing. Like so many sensational stories throughout human history, this association is the stuff of which myths are made. Neither man ever robbed a grave. They were, not body snatchers, but something even worse: cold-blooded murderers.

Irish Catholics who moved to Edinburgh (Burke in 1818; Hare during the mid-1820s), both men originally sought navy work, but joined forces when Burke and his mistress, Helen MacDougal, moved into Log's, a boarding house in Tanner's Close owned by Hare and his wife. Burke and MacDougal had met Hare at Penicuik, south of Edinburgh, where they were all working during harvest time. At Log's, both couples enjoyed pursuing a raucous, alcohol-fueled lifestyle.

When a lodger named Donald died in the house on November 29, 1827, Hare teamed with Burke to sell the body to Dr. Knox, who, experiencing a dearth in dissection subjects, paid them the ample sum of £7 10s. Subsequently, they murdered 16 people, delivering the corpses to Knox. The victims, often female, were either lodgers or locals lured with the promise of liquor and sex. The method of murder involved a suffocation technique which left no detectable signs of violence on the body. In his 1995 book *Murdering to Dissect*, Tim Marshall notes, "Burke and Hare took graverobbing to its logical conclusion: instead of digging up the dead, they accepted lucrative incentives to destroy the living."[1]

Two candidates have been identified as possibly being the first murder victim: a miller named Joseph, who also was living at Log's; or Abigail Simpson, a local salt seller. Some historians and commentators, including Sir Walter Scott, have leaned toward Joseph, who was smothered with a pillow. Delirious from a high fever, Joseph, considered dangerously infectious by the Hares, was plied with whisky before the deadly deed was done: While Burke immobilized the victim by laying across his torso, Hare applied the fatal pillow to his face. Knox awarded them with the princely sum of £10 for a specimen in such fine physical condition, insured in part by the suffocation method of murder, the cause of death being virtually imperceptible to any investigator at the time. Knox, impressed by the "freshness" of the corpses, continued to pay them, £8 to £10 for each, while asking no questions about the method of procurement.

One of the duo's victims, Mary Paterson [aka "Mary Mitchell"], whom they murdered after she passed out from overindulgence, was recognized by an anatomy student named Fergusson, who received the body, which they had stuffed inside a tea-chest. When questioned about the still-warm corpse, Burke replied that, after she had died from "the drink," they purchased it from an elderly woman in the Canongate district of central Edinburgh. Over the next three months, Knox, who paid £8 for the delivery, stored the corpse in a vat of whisky. Strongly affected by the dead girl's stunning appearance, several students sketched her form before Knox performed the dissection. Knox's knowledge of the Paterson murder and that of James Wilson [aka "Daft Jamie"], a well-known mentally disabled, homeless Edinburgh teenager referred to as a "half-wit," weighed heavily against him after Burke and Hare were arrested.

Subsequent victims, female lodgers killed in the house or the nearby stable, all after being befuddled with whisky, were delivered in the tea-chest to Knox. One of their efforts, in June 1828, involved a double murder, that of an old woman and her deaf-mute grandson, whom Burke later confessed expired with a hideous expression that troubled him greatly.[2] Delivering two victims together proved a challenge for the murderous team, who abandoned the tea-chest for a herring barrel, into which they were forced to press the corpses, fetching £8 each from Knox. Further trouble had occurred on the way to Surgeon's Square, when the horse pulling Hare's cart halted at the Grassmarket, where he found a porter to help transport the container of death the remaining distance atop a handcart. Back at Tanner's Close, Hare vented his psychotic rage by executing the horse.

On June 24, when Burke and McDougal travelled to Falkirk to visit her father, Hare decided to commit a solo murder, from which he used a portion of the £8 payment to purchase a new wardrobe. When he lied to Burke about the deed, Hare incited an argument, culminating in a fistfight and the Burkes' relocation to the nearby home of a cousin named Broggan [or "Brogan"].

Three months later, the duo, resuming their homicidal collaboration, killed a washerwoman who had arrived at Log's to do her laundry. The £8 netted from the delivery was split evenly this time around. Not long after, they committed another murder, during a visit by Ann Dougal [McDougal], one of Helen's Falkirk relatives, for whom they were awarded £10. Burke later confessed that he rejected a suggestion by Hare's wife that Helen also be killed, on grounds that a "Scotch woman" could not be trusted.[3]

"Daft Jamie," just 18 years old, his mental illness compounded with a limping gait caused by a deformation of the feet, had resorted to begging while living on the streets. One November day, Hare easily baited the lad with the usual promise of whisky, sending his wife to fetch Burke as soon as they arrived at the lodgings. In one of the bedrooms, Jamie imbibed only a small amount of alcohol; and, when the substitution of snuff did not elicit the usual effect, he fought back ferociously when the two men attempted to subdue and suffocate him. Finally overpowering him, they carried out their usual modus operandi, stripped his body, and stole his snuff box and spoon. Following delivery, Knox and several students recognized the "daft" lad, and word of his "disappearance" began to be whispered in the streets. Knox decapitated and amputated the feet from the corpse, which he then prioritized on his list of dissection subjects.

The 16th murder, coincidentally, was carried out during the evening of October 31, 1828. Burke lured Mary Docherty, a middle-aged Irish pauper, into the Broggan lodging house, where, claiming that his mother might be a member of the woman's family, broke out the *uisge-beatha* ["water of life"]. When the supply ran low, Burke, citing a need to fetch additional refreshments, left Helen MacDougal in charge while he ran out to locate Hare. During the Halloween festivities, around 9 p.m., Ann and James Gray, a couple also lodging at Broggan's, witnessed the drunken carousing of Burke, Hare, their wives and Docherty. Following yet another fistfight, the killers reconciled long enough to suffocate the inebriated mendicant, hide her naked body beneath some straw under a bed, and then douse the room with ample whisky to disguise the anticipated stench.

The Grays, who had slept at Log's that night, returned the following day. Worried by Docherty's unexplained absence, Mrs. Gray became suspicious when Burke refused to let her collect a pair of stockings she had left on the bed. That evening, when the others stepped out, she and her husband discovered the corpse, the face of which displayed both saliva and blood. Venturing toward the nearest police station, they were intercepted by Helen MacDougal, who, in vain, offered a bribe of £10 for their silence. While they reported the murder, Burke and Hare quickly transported the corpse to Knox's surgery. But, being Saturday night, the laboratory was closed, so they left the tea-chest in the cellar. Knox gave them £5, agreeing to pay the balance following a Monday examination.[4]

Arriving at Broggan's, the police found Docherty's abandoned clothing, stained with blood, stuffed under the bed.[5] When questioned, Burke and his wife both gave differing accounts, including the time of Docherty's "departure from the house." The next morning, the police discovered Docherty's corpse at Knox's surgery, where James Gray identified it as "the woman he had seen" celebrating with Burke and Hare. Hare, his wife, and Broggan were arrested, all denying any knowledge of the events.[6]

On November 3, a detention warrant was served on Burke, Hare, and their wives, while Broggan was released from custody. The suspects, confined separately, all gave conflicting statements, differing from those they had made at the time of arrest. The police surgeon's examination of Docherty's body was supplemented by those of two forensic specialists, Robert Christison and William Newbigging, who agreed that murder by suffocation was "probable" but could not be proved medically.[7] The report, however, provided enough evidence on which to charge both Burke and Hare with murder.[8] Christison, a toxicologist and physician at the Royal Infirmary of Edinburgh (and later served as president of the Royal College of Physicians of Edinburgh and the British Medical Association, respectively), carried his investigation beyond an autopsy. When questioning Dr. Knox, he was told that Burke and Hare were not "resurrection men," but rather those who bought corpses from operators of lodging houses before they could be claimed for burial. Christison reported to the authorities that he considered Knox "deficient in principle and heart" but not criminally responsible.[9]

Concerned with the lack of corroborating evidence (specifically the non-existence of *corpus delicti* in the other suspected murders), the police were in doubt about securing a conviction in the case. As the public grapevine spread sensational accounts involving Mary Paterson and "Daft Jamie," local residents informed the authorities of seeing clothing they had been known to wear. On November 19, a second warrant, charging the four suspects with the murder of James Wilson, also was issued.

Sir William Rae, Lord Advocate, sought obtaining a confession from one of the four suspects, who could be persuaded to turn king's evidence in exchange for a promise of immunity from prosecution. Hare was more than game, making a full confession of all 16 deaths, satisfying Rae that he had sufficient evidence for a successful prosecution. On December 4, formal charges were filed against William Burke and Helen MacDougal for the murders of Mary Paterson, James Wilson and Mary Docherty.

Knox, exonerated by Burke's previous statement, was not charged in the case, although public opinion was greatly set against him. Newspapers and broadsides indicated the extent of Edinburghians' disgust for the anatomist, with editorials expressing the view that he, too, should have stood in the dock beside Burke and McDougal. In fact, the term "burking" became a popular way to describe murdering a victim by suffocation. Chapbook sellers and street singers also circulated popular rhymes referring to Burke and Hare's iniquitous exploits.

Holidays continued to figure into the chronology of the Burke and Hare murder case. At 10 a.m. on December 24, 1828, the High Court of Justiciary in Edinburgh's Parliament House, was called to a Christmas Eve order by Lord Justice-Clerk David Boyel, supported by Lords Meadowbank, Pitmilly and Mackenzie. The large courtroom had begun filling to capacity an hour earlier, and a force of 300 constables, with infantry and cavalry troops placed on standby, assembled to police the even larger gathering outside the building.

Following objections from the defense counsel, Rae split the indictment into separate charges for each of the three murders, choosing first to hear the Docherty case. In this instance, the prosecution held the strongest evidence, including the body of the victim.[10] Burke and McDougal pleaded not guilty, and witnesses began to be called from a long list (of 55, but not all testified). Knox provided testimony, but he and three of his assistants avoided being questioned in open court. One assistant, David Paterson, confirmed that both Burke and Hare had delivered and accepted payment for several subjects.

That evening, Hare took the stand and, during cross-examination, identified Burke as the "sole murderer" and McDougal as being "twice involved" in escorting Docherty back into the house after she had scurried out during the Halloween party. He also admitted to assisting in delivering the corpse to Knox's surgery.[11] Hare's wife also was called, but used their ill infant as a distraction while claiming a "poor memory" was responsible for her inability to answer questions satisfactorily.[12]

Final witnesses for the prosecution were Alexander Black, the police surgeon, and Robert Christison, both admitting suspicion of foul play but also that no forensic evidence supported a conclusion of mur-

William Burke, by George Andrew Lutenor, a juror at Burke's 1828 trial.

William Hare, by George Andrew Lutenor, a juror at Burke's 1828 trial.

der. No defense witnesses appeared, with pre-trial declarations from Burke and MacDougal being substituted.

At 3 a.m. on Christmas morning, Burke and McDougal's defense attorneys followed the prosecutorial summation. Boyle then provided his summary, directing the jury to accept the arguments of the prosecution. At 8:30 a.m., the jurors retired to consider the verdicts, which they delivered a mere 50 minutes later. Burke was found guilty for the murder of Docherty, but the equal charge against McDougal was declared "not proven." (Outside Scotland, this is often called the "Scottish verdict," while the Scots themselves occasionally give tongue to "bastard verdict," a colloquial term coined by Sir Walter Scott.)

Boyle sentenced Burke to death by hanging. Included in the sentence was a standard component suffered by all convicted murderers:

Sir Robert Cristison, a toxicologist and physician at the Royal Infirmary of Edinburgh, testified at William Burke's 1828 trial that the forensic examination of Mary Doherty's corpse revealed "probable" death by suffocation, but also that no evidence supported a conclusion of murder.

"anatomisation."[13] This provision was part of The Murder Act [of] 1751, passed into law by the Parliament of Great Britain "for better preventing the horrid crime of murder."[14] Intended to add "further terror and [a] peculiar mark of infamy" to the punishment of a murderer, it mandated that the body, "in no case whatsoever [would] be suffered to be buried."[15] Instead, the executed criminal would either be dissected or hanged in chains publicly.

McDougal was released from custody and, after returning to Log's, was confronted by an angry mob as she went out to buy whisky. Escorted by police to Fountainbridge, she was forced by another gang to escape from the police building into Edinburgh's High Street. Refused permission to visit Burke, she fled the Scottish capital into obscurity the following day.

Advised by Catholic and Protestant clergymen, Burke made a more detailed confession on January 3, 1829, laying much of the blame for the murders on Hare. Two weeks later, James Wilson's mother filed a petition calling for a revocation of Hare's immunity and intended release from prison, but the High Court of Justiciary rejected it by a 4 to 2 vote. On January 18, Margaret Hare was released, subsequently leaving for Glasgow, where she was attacked by a mob while awaiting her sea voyage back to Ireland. Police aided her in boarding a ship bound for Belfast, where she, too, drifted into anonymity.

On January 28, 1829, the hangman ended the earthly existence of William Burke. A substantial number of spectators, amid a crowd estimated at 25,000, loudly chanted, "*Burke* him!" before the body dropped. Customarily, inhabitants of the surrounding tenements rented viewing space from their windows at prices ranging from five to 25 shillings.

The aftermath of the hanging promised to rival the gruesomeness of the murders. Some in the gathering and a group of students nearly incited a riot by demanding access to the ticketed lecture scheduled to follow the execution. Flaring tempers were calmed when one of the university professors promised admittance to groups of 50 who would be allowed to view the results of the dissection. During the procedure, which lasted for two hours, Alexander Monro, then serving as chairman of the Anatomy Department at Edinburgh University, thrust his quill pen into Burke's head, from which he used the murderer's blood to write confirmation of the execution and dissection. Placed in the Anatomical Museum of the Edinburgh Medical School, Burke's skeleton remains on display two centuries later.

For his own protection, Hare remained in police custody until February 5, 1829, after which he was escorted, incognito, via mail coach more than 60 miles southward to Dumfries. Threatened by organized vigilante mobs, he hid out in the town prison. When stones were hurled at streetlamps, and then the building's door and windows, 100 constables were called to restore order. The next morning, a militia guard sneaked him out of Dumfries. Turned loose on the Annan Road, he was ordered by a sheriff to make for the English border. He apparently crossed into northern England, where the last known sighting of his fleeing form occurred on a road near Carlisle. Like the fates of his and Burke's female partners, William Hare's ultimate destiny remains a mystery. Interestingly, the sole corporeal remains that may be visited today are those of Burke, the only individual found guilty in the serial spree of 16 murders.

Three years after the conclusion of the Burke and Hare case, a new anatomy bill was passed by the House of Lords on July 19, 1832. The principal provision of the Anatomy Act stipulated that a person having lawful possession of a body could grant permission, barring objection from a confirmed relative, for an "anatomical examination" to be performed. The act was devised to benefit physicians, surgeons and students by granting access to unclaimed corpses, particularly of those who had died in a hospital, prison or workhouse.[16] Public participation was encouraged by allowing anatomy schools to pay for burials in exchange for donations by next of kin. Persons interested in "the advancement of science" also could leave their own bodies for dissection, provided that no relatives objected after the donor's demise.

Having made no public statements about Burke and Hare, Dr. Knox, vilified in print and burned in effigy by a crowd outside his home, was officially cleared of complicity in the crimes. He eventually resigned from the museum of the College of Surgeons and left Edinburgh in 1842. Failing to attract new students in Glasgow, where his career slowed to a near standstill, he focused on lecturing throughout Great Britain and mainland Europe. In London, he was forbidden to lecture after violating the regulations of the Royal College of Surgeons. Two years later, he published the dubious book *Races of Men*, indicating that he studied anatomy in the hope of proving the superiority of the Scandinavian race. A pre-Darwinian believer in the "survival of the fittest" philosophy, Knox was "the real founder of British racism and one of the key figures in the general Western movement toward a dogmatic pseudo-scientific racism."[17]

Much like his attitude toward the "dark races"—"Destined by the nature of their race to run like all other animals, a certain limited course of existence, it matters little how their extinction is brought about"—Knox believed that murdering "useless" individuals was a humane practice.[18] Scottish historian Owen Dudley Edwards notes, "Knox simply did not regard the Burke and Hare murders as criminal: on the contrary, he looked on them as an enlightened method of disposing of worthless individuals with the ultimate betterment to the more desirable segments of humanity by reason of the benefits conferred to the study of anatomy."[19]

Knox finally secured another medical position in 1856, as a pathological anatomist at the Brompton Cancer Hospital, and ran his own practice in Hackney, where he died six years later. (Shortly before his demise, he revised *Races of Men*, attempting to provide a defense for some accusations levelled at the "much maligned races," specifically South African Blacks.) Though some biographers have drawn attention to his important contributions to the study of anatomy, as well as transcendentalism and evolution, his views on race and involvement with Burke and Hare have overshadowed his achievements. Over the years, Edinburgh tour guides have readily pointed out the location of his laboratory and the nearby graveyard from which several bodies were reportedly stolen. None, however, were disinterred by Burke and Hare, who selected all their subjects from life.

2

Young Robert Louis Stevenson and "The Body-Snatcher"

THE LITERARY OUTPUT of Robert Lewis Balfour Stevenson reflects the singular nature of his life. His love of "clean, open air adventure" was engendered by the vivid imagination he developed as a frail child. During his later wayfaring efforts to forestall the death that chronic illness would bring, he evolved into one of the most original and versatile writers in the English language.

Stevenson was born November 13, 1850, at 8 Howard Place in Edinburgh. The only child of Thomas and Margaret Isabella Balfour Stevenson, Lewis (as he was called throughout his life) spent his early years "amid elegant streets inhabited by genteel professional families."[1]

Born in 1818, Thomas Stevenson had followed in the footsteps of his father, Robert Stevenson (1772-1850), a successful engineer who developed many innovations for the lighthouses of Scotland. Thomas extended his father's work by devising new methods of illumination allowing navigators to steer safer courses into port, particularly through the narrow Irish Sea. In 1853, he became joint engineer for the Board of Northern Lights, a post he successfully maintained until 1885.

The "Robert" in young Stevenson's name was a tribute to Robert Stevenson, who died a few months before he was born, and "Lewis" honored Lewis Balfour, Margaret's father. Some years later, the spelling of Lewis was changed to "Louis." One theory suggests that Thomas, a strict Calvinist and Tory, made the change after a radical Edinburgh

Birthplace of Robert Louis Stevenson, 8 Howard Place, Edinburgh (September 1990 photo by Scott Allen Nollen).

politician named Lewis offended him. (The French pronunciation of *Louis*, with a silent "s," was never used.)

Tiny and physically underdeveloped, Louis was given the colloquial Scots nickname *Smout* by his parents, who likened his size to that of a "small fry" salmon. From age two, he suffered from various maladies, particularly coughs and fevers that developed into bronchial infections. Referred to as a "lung weakness," this predisposition was inherited from the Balfours, who had a history of respiratory disorders. Lewis and Margaret experienced attacks of coughing and chills, and these problems were passed on to the young Louis, who spent much of his first nine years in bed. Also troubled by gastric infections, he often suffered from insomnia and was forced to rely on a vivid imagination to pass the long night-time hours. Reinforced by stories recited by his nurse, Alison Cunningham, who was hired when Louis was 18 months old, his creative impulses evolved at a prodigious rate. By age six, he began dictating essays to his mother.

Margaret's ancestors, the Balfours of Pilrig (located between Edinburgh's Old Town and Leith), were a landed family of substantial means who had contributed to major events in Scottish history. In 1679, when the Presbyterian Covenanters rebelled against the religious intolerance of King Charles II, a Balfour fought at Bothwell Brig, the decisive battle during which the Duke of Monmouth's forces crushed the uprising.

At age nine, Louis protested about the *Smout* moniker, demanding a fine of one penny from anyone who spoke it aloud. Thereafter, Thomas and Margaret both called him "Lou," and the diminutive stuck. During family holidays on the Berwickshire coast, he enjoyed capering amid the sea and sand, playing pirates and treasure hunters with other lads his age. Visits to Allan Water, near Stirling, and the battlefields of Bannockburn and Sherriffmuir increased his interest in Scotland's turbulent history.

Educated at schools in Edinburgh and Isleworth, Middlesex, he supplemented formal studies by continuing to develop and dictate his own ideas and stories, often to "Cummy," who recorded them in her

Edinburgh Castle (September 1990 photo by Scott Allen Nollen).

diary. During the autumn of 1863, he accompanied Thomas on a tour of lighthouses along the coast of Fife. Two years later, he repeated the experience when they sailed up the coast to Wick Harbor in the eastern Highlands. In late 1867, he was accepted by Edinburgh University, where Thomas expected him to gear his studies toward the family tradition of lighthouse and harbor engineering. Realizing that his son was too frail for such a physically demanding vocation, he allowed him to study for the bar, but Louis spent far more time reading Scottish history, French literature, and the controversial works of thinkers such as Herbert Spencer and Charles Darwin.

Far from accepting Thomas' genteel thinking, Louis expressed himself in ways that were "disturbingly iconoclastic."[2] He sought an escape from the conventional lifestyle prized by Edinburgh's upper class, his initial rebellion represented by wearing odd attire and frequenting the taverns and *howffs* on the Water of Leith, where he interacted with beggars, criminals and prostitutes. His growing familiarity with philosophical and fictional literature may have inspired him to seek such company, but his interest in Scotland's historical rebels also had a strong impact. In a short time, many respectable people became used to seeing the thin, gleaming-eyed Louis striding through the streets, sporting a black shirt and neckerchief under a garish velvet jacket, and speaking in strange, decorous language.

His period of revolt was due in part to the stage of rebelliousness experienced by many youths during the late teen years, but as Victorian scholar David Daiches suggests, youthful passion was not the sole component:

> There was more than one crisis between Stevenson and his family which left its mark on both father and son. When Stevenson embraced the bohemian way of life it was not a fad but a profession of faith... an attitude and a way of life which he had come to believe in as a result of much genuine heart-searching and a great deal of very real unhappiness.[3]

Scottish historian Moray McLaren explained,

> Eccentricities—those like deep drinking, running after loose women were all habits that could be allowed to the established and the middle-aged in a quite prosaic fashion. They must not, however, be romanticized. Young men, as the wiseacres of mid-Victorian Edinburgh knew, were inclined to invest their irregularities with a specious romance, even to sentimentalize them.....It was not... permitted for the young men of the city to imitate their elders.....It was in such an atmosphere that the young Robert Louis Stevenson began his career of eccentricity and bohemianism. All Edinburgh, both the conventional and the permittedly unconventional, were naturally opposed to him. It was only in the true underworld, amongst the unselfconsciously unconventional, that Robert Louis Stevenson of the velvet coat was accepted without question.[4]

Stevenson's bohemianism found little support among his cohorts at the university. Many students considered unconventional attitudes a waste of time, an offensive practice that detracted from a proper education. Biographer Jenni Calder explained,

> In Scotland, university education had traditionally been open to the sons of families that in England had never dreamt of the possibility. For that reason, learning was regarded with the greatest respect and seriousness. Stevenson's irresponsible, cavalier attitude, his scoffing at precisely the authorities and institutions that offered opportunities for achievement to the poor but decent, was not popular.[5]

During the summers of 1869 and 1870, Louis joined his father on voyages amid the Orkney and Hebridean islands, and their three-week stay on the tidal islet of Earraid during the latter trip would eventually inform two of his finest Scottish stories. In 1870, he also renewed a friendship with his cousin, Bob Stevenson, an art student and social activist at Cambridge, who exerted a strong influence over him.

In early 1873, Thomas was shocked to find the written constitution of the "Liberty, Justice, and Reverence" society among Louis' documents. Created by Bob Stevenson, this anti-establishment organization required its members to "disregard everything our parents have taught us." Thomas' discovery of the manifesto led to a discussion of religion and the realization that his son was, in his words, a "horrible atheist." Never one to hold extremist opinions, Louis instead formulated a rational agnosticism. David Daiches reported,

> Louis tried to explain his ideas about the difference between morality and religious institutions and to persuade his father that he accepted the ideals of Christian morality while repudiating the Church and behaviour of most people who called themselves Christians. But his parents were touched on a most sensitive spot, and the thought that their son was an infidel was beyond the reach of rational distinctions.[6]

During this time, Louis began expressing his views on Victorian social conventions in poetical form:

> I am a hunchback, yellow faced,—
>   A hateful sight to see,—
> 'Tis all that other men can do
>   To pass and let me be.
> I am a woman,—my hair is white—
>   I was a drunkard's lass;
> The gin dances in my head,—
>   I stumble as I pass.
> I am a man that God made at first,
>   And teachers tried to harm;
> Here, hunchback, take my friendly hand,—
>   Good woman, take my arm.

Stevenson's recognition of the ambiguous nature of human behavior and morality would serve him well when he began to write fiction professionally during the late 1870s.

During the summer of 1876, Louis accompanied Bob Stevenson to France, where he met Francis ["Fanny"] Matilda Van de Grift Osbourne, an Indiana-born 35-year-old, separated from her husband, who was vacationing at Grez-sur-Loing with her two children, teenage Isobel and seven-year-old Lloyd. At this stage in his career, Louis had been writing literary essays and reviews for about three years. From the time of his first published work in the December 1873 issue of *The Portfolio* to his acquaintance with Fanny Osbourne less than three years later, he had completed approximately 20 pieces for periodicals such as *Cornhill Magazine*, *The Academy*, *Vanity Fair* and *MacMillan's Magazine*. By his mid-twenties, he already had displayed elements of the diversity that would distinguish his later fictional efforts. He wrote of Scottish topography, history and song, the works of great authors from both sides of the Atlantic, and offered his views on idleness, friendship, relations between the sexes, and other social topics.

The subject of his first book-length work, *An Inland Voyage* (1878), was provided by a September-October 1876 canoe trip on the canals of Belgium and France with his friend, Walter Simpson. After joining Fanny and Lloyd in Paris that autumn, he returned to Edinburgh.

In early 1877, the short story "An Old Song" (originally titled "The Two Falconers of Cairnstane") became his first published fictional work when it appeared anonymously in *London* magazine. That summer, he returned to France and, in September, joined the Osbournes in Paris. On July 27, he was back in Scotland, lodging with his parents at Swanston, a two-story cottage in the Pentland Hills, which Thomas had been leasing since the summer of 1867. During agreeable weather, Louis often enjoyed walking through the braes to meet friends in Edinburgh. On this occasion, he had returned from France to attend his friend Charles Baxter's wedding.

Until August 1878, when Fanny left Paris for her California home, Louis spent considerable time on French holidays, either with the Osbournes or seeking "legitimate" work. During a Paris International Exhibition held in June 1878, he served as secretary to Edinburgh University Professor of Engineering [Henry Charles] Fleeming Jenkin, inventor of the telpherage (cable car).

Louis continued writing fiction, selling stories such as "Will o' the Mill" and "The Sire de Maletroit's Door" to various periodicals. *An In-*

> Swanston
> Friday.
>
> Dear Sir,
>
> My father is from home on business and doesnot return till Saturday evening; so it will be impossible for him to attend the funeral of your mother. I know he will regret this much, for we all liked and respected Mrs Young. You may be sure that we sympathise with you on your loss. Swanston has never looked itself since your good father was taken hence; and now here is another link gone. But at least it is agreeable to think that husband and wife are now reunited after a very brief separation.
>
> Yours very truly
> Robert Louis Stevenson
>
> R. Young Esq.

Robert Louis Stevenson, letter to Robert Young, son of the family's late gardener, Swanston cottage, Pentland Hills, July 27, 1877.

land Voyage was published in May 1878 and soon was followed by similar travelogues documenting his experiences in Scotland and France. On August 7, 1879, he sailed from Greenock on a voyage to Monterey, California, where the Osbournes were expecting his arrival. For 10 days, he observed the many immigrants from Great Britain, Ireland and mainland Europe who populated the ship's steerage. *The Amateur Emigrant*, his written narrative of the journey (later to be published in periodical and book versions), features documentary accounts that would influence his fictional works, including *Kidnapped*.

He arrived in New York nine days later, and following a river boat ride to Jersey City, began an 11-day rail journey with immigrants crossing the United States for the first time. His lack of social prejudice was demonstrated by "his readiness to muck in with any of his working-class fellows on boat or train, his passionate and almost childlike interest in them, and his acceptance of them as his equals."[7] He was offended by the way his fellow Caucasians treated the members of non-white races, particularly the Chinese, who were being accused of spreading a foul odor throughout the train. In *The Amateur Emigrant*, he emphasizes the "dexterity and frugality" of the Chinese, while judging Caucasians to be "lazy [and] luxurious." He also was disgusted by the derision aimed at Native Americans. After hearing his fellow passengers mock "the noble red man of the old story," he "was ashamed for the thing we call civilization."

Three weeks of cramped and dusty travel were capped by his arrival in Monterey at the end of August. The reason for his presence at the Osbourne household, although under Fanny's cover story that her "literary friend from Scotland has accepted an engagement to come to America and lecture," was apparent, especially to the children. His obvious love for Fanny, however, was complicated by his poor health, which had been exacerbated by the frantic, unsanitary nature of the journey, during which irregular sleep, bad weather and lack of nutritious food had worsened his sensitive bronchial condition.

Louis continued to write, jotting down copious notes about his experiences in San Francisco and completing essays on Henry David Thoreau, Benjamin Franklin and Sir William Penn. He also began an autobiography and composed the first draft of his famous poem "Requiem":

> Under the wide and starry sky,
> Dig the grave and let me lie.
> Glad did I live and gladly die,
> And I laid me down with a will.
> This be the verse you grave for me:
> *Here he lies where he longed to be,*
> *Here is the sailor, home from sea,*
> *And the hunter home from the hill.*

While lodging in an Oakland hotel, Louis experienced a serious lung haemorrhage. Following this incident, he "lived for the rest of his life under the threat of recurrence, a threat in fact of sudden death."[8] Several medical professionals agreed that he suffered from tuberculosis, but the actual illness was never pinpointed with certainty. To be safe, Louis, aided considerably by Fanny's faithful nursing, lived as if he were tubercular, referring to the malady as "Bluidy Jack." To better monitor his condition, Fanny moved him into the parlor of her cottage. Considering the financial burden imposed by marriage, he was relieved by a missive from Thomas, who offered an annual allowance of £250.

On May 19, 1880, Louis and Fanny were wed at the San Francisco home of Reverend William A. Scott, a Scottish Presbyterian minister. Indulging their adventurous spirits, they honeymooned near the Calistoga Gold and Silver Mine at Silverado in California's Napa Valley until the end of July. Excited by the location, Louis documented their experiences in a journal called *The Silverado Squatters* (eventually revised and published in 1883).

In early August, Louis, Fanny and Lloyd boarded a Pullman train bound for New York, initiating his return to Scotland following a one-year absence. On August 17, they disembarked from the ship *City of Chester* in Liverpool. Back in Scotland in September, they joined Louis' parents for a brief holiday in the Highlands, where he met with Principal John Tulloch of St. Andrews University. Interested in making good use of his lifelong interest in his country's history, he proposed writing a nonfiction book called "Scotland and the Union: The Transformation of the Scottish Highlands." Though he penned a draft, highlighting "what he believed to be key events and charac-

Robert Louis Stevenson, at the time of his marriage, shortly before he wrote "The Body-Snatcher," 1880.

ters of 18th century Highland history," the book was left uncompleted. As explained by Lachlan Munro, "Stevenson's career was littered with abandoned projects… [the book] was too ambitious for a writer who hitherto had been an essayist and a poet, but, it might be added, particularly one who, as a bohemian urbanite, had no real understanding of the Highlands, and who had no Gaelic."[9]

Back in Edinburgh, Louis sought various ways to improve his ill health. During the winter of 1880-1881, he took Fanny and Lloyd to Davos, Switzerland, where a new resort area had been established for consumptives. At the end of April, they returned to Scotland and, during the summer, stayed with Louis' parents in rented cottages at Pitlochry and Braemar, near Balmoral, in Aberdeenshire, where the novel *Treasure Island* was conceived.

At his father's request, Louis applied for a legitimate position at Edinburgh University when the chair of history and constitutional law became vacant in 1881. He lacked the necessary qualifications, but the gesture pleased Thomas and reflected his "real and increasing interest in Scottish history."[10]

The summer of 1881 proved to be a literarily terrifying one for Louis. Engulfed in Highland Rain at Pitlochry, he wrote three Scottish stories, all powerful thrillers, in picturesque Kinnaird Cottage, where he and Fanny enjoyed a roaring fire and the ghoulish folk tales of Mrs. Sim, their hostess. In June he completed "Thrawn Janet" (his only story entirely in the Scots language [Lallans]) and began "The Body-Snatcher" and "The Merry Men," both of which occupied him well into the following month.

Incorporating memories of his summers spent in the Pentland Hills with his knowledge of sensational events occurring a half-century earlier, he developed the fact-inspired tale that became "The Body-Snatcher." Upon completing the story in July 1881, he initially thought it "too horrid" for publication.[11]

In Stevenson's 1878 essay collection "Edinburgh: Picturesque Notes," chapter five ("Greyfriars") includes his comment that the Scots "stand…highest among the nations in the matter of grimly illustrating death":

> We seem to love for their own sake the emblems of time and the great change; and even around country churches you will find a wonderful exhibition of skulls, and crossbones, and noseless angels, and trumpets pealing for the Judgement Day. Every mason was a pedestrian Holbein: he had a deep consciousness of death, and loved to put its terrors pithily before the churchyard loiterer; he was brim-

ful of rough hints upon mortality, and any dead farmer was seized upon to be a text.

Louis had heard folk retellings of the notorious murders of 1828-1829 all his life, and he researched the subject for "Edinburgh: Picturesque Notes." In chapter four ("Legends"), he writes, "... people hush their voices over Burke and Hare; over drugs and violated graves, and the resurrection-men smothering their victims with their knees." Opening the chapter, he explains, "The character of a place is often most perfectly expressed in its associations. An event strikes root and grows into a legend, when it has happened amongst congenial surroundings. Ugly actions, above all in ugly places, have the true romantic quality, and become an undying property of their scene."

He vividly describes such an "ugly" scene in "Greyfriars":

Gravestone, Melrose Abbey, Roxburghshire, Borders: "... even around country churches you will find a wonderful exhibition of skulls, and crossbones...." (September 1990 photo by Scott Allen Nollen).

I shall never forget one visit. It was a grey, dropping day; the grass was strung with raindrops; and the people in the houses kept hanging out their shirts and petticoats and angrily taking them in again, as the weather turned from wet to fair and back again. A gravedigger, and a friend of his, a gardener from the country, accompanied me into one after another of the cells and little courtyards in which it gratified the wealthy of old days to enclose their old bones from neighbourhood. In one, under a sort of shrine, we found a forlorn human effigy, very realistically executed down to the detail of his ribbed stockings, and holding in his hand a ticket with the date of his demise. He looked most pitiful and ridiculous, shut up by himself in his aristocratic precinct, like a bad old boy or an inferior forgotten deity under a new dispensation; the burdocks grew familiarly about his feet, the rain dripped all round him; and the world maintained the most entire indifference as to who he was or whither he had gone. In another, a vaulted tomb, handsome externally but horrible inside with damp and cobwebs, there were three mounds of black earth and an uncovered thigh bone. This was the place of internment, it appeared, of a family with whom the gardener had been long in service. He was among old acquaintances. "This'll be Miss Margaret's," said he, giving the bone a friendly kick. "The auld—!" I have always an uncomfortable feeling in a graveyard, at sight of so many tombs to perpetuate memories best forgotten; but I never had the impression so strongly as that day. People had been at some expense in both these cases: to provoke a melancholy feeling of derision in the one, and an insulting epithet in the other. The proper inscription for the most part of mankind, I began to think, is the cynical jeer, *crastibi*. That, if anything, will stop the mouth of a carper; since it both admits the worst and carries the war triumphantly into the enemy's camp.

He directly follows this recollection with another mention (more legendary than factual) of a certain executed killer:

Greyfriars is a place of many associations. There was one window in a house at the lower end, now demolished, which was pointed out to me by the gravedigger as a spot of legendary interest. Burke, the resurrection man, infamous for so many murders at five shillings a head, used to sit thereat, with pipe and nightcap, to watch burials going forward on the green.

The 1879 edition of "Edinburgh: Picturesque Notes" concludes with the chapter "Into the Pentland Hills." Along with Edinburgh and environs, another location Stevenson chose to utilize in "The Body-Snatcher" was a churchyard in the area of the Pentland Hills with which he was quite familiar. The parish of Glencorse was founded in 1616 by combining the ancient parishes of Pentland and Penicuik. After the original kirk burned down, a new building was constructed in 1665. At the time Stevenson wrote "The Body-Snatcher," the kirk was still in use, but was superseded for worship by a larger new parish church in

"The Pentland Hills from Swanston," painted by James Heron for chapter 10, "To the Pentland Hills," in "Edinburgh--Picturesque Notes" (1879; 1914 edition).

Glencorse kirk, erected in 1885, postdates "The Body-Snatcher" by four years (September 1990 photo by Scott Allen Nollen).

1885. Thereafter, the 1665 building became known as Glencorse Old Kirk.

Penicuik is also the location of the Fishers Tryst tavern and rustic kirkyard where the body-snatching characters of Macfarlane and Fettes hide their gravedigging implements in the story. The Glencorse

"Burying Ground of the People of Glencorse" (September 1990 photo by Scott Allen Nollen).

churches and graveyard are located up the hill from the tryst. And the name "Fettes" graces at least four sites in Edinburgh, including Fettes Row, a street situated between Howard Place and Heriot Row that was familiar to Stevenson. (Professor and Mrs. Fleeming Jenkin settled on Fettes Row when they moved to Edinburgh in 1868.)

Stevenson's 11th completed fictional work to be published, "The Body-Snatcher" was shelved for three and one-half years before it was included in the December 1884 *Pall Mall Christmas Extra*. Appearing on the scene shortly after the success of *Treasure Island*, first published in book form in November 1883, it was dismissed as a piece of sensationalistic horror. Although the story rarely progresses beyond a sketch of two characters involved in a specific series of events, it provides a fictionalized portrait of the grisly crimes that shocked Edinburgh and much of Great Britain in 1828-1829.

Penicuik old kirk and cemetery (September 1990 photo by Scott Allen Nollen).

The Fishers Tryst, 35 Milton Bridge, Penicuik (September 1990 photograph by Scott Allen Nollen).

The Published Tale

Donald Fettes, an aging, rum-swilling Scotsman (Stevenson uses the period term "Scotchman"), sits with three friends in the parlor of the George Inn at Debenham. When Dr. Wolfe Macfarlane arrives to treat a neighbour, Fettes comes face-to-face with an old acquaintance. "Toddy Macfarlane!" he shouts, surprising the doctor, who offers the hospitality of his Edinburgh home. Fettes refuses, whispering, "Have you seen it again?" Aghast, Macfarlane cries out, strikes Fettes across the face, and flees the inn.

Intrigued by the meeting, Fettes' companions investigate his past associations with the "great rich London doctor." In a flashback describing Fettes' "young days," he is shown as a talented medical student in the schools of Edinburgh. As an assistant in the dissection laboratory of Dr. K---, he is influenced by Dr. Macfarlane, his immediate superior and aide in K---'s anatomy class. Together, they accept "subjects" for dissection from "resurrection men" who call during the dark hours of the night. Admitting that the subjects are being murdered due to a short supply of cadavers, Macfarlane kills Gray, an associate in body-snatching. Warned not to reveal this secret, Fettes distributes Gray's "parts" for student dissection.

On a pitch black and stormy night, Fettes and Macfarlane disinter a woman's corpse in an old graveyard at Glencorse. Driving back to Edinburgh, they are made uneasy by the body, which continually falls against them as the gig careens on the wet, windswept road. "This is not a woman," Macfarlane frantically declares as Fettes holds a lantern up to the corpse's face. Screaming out in fright, both men abandon the gig as the lantern crashes to the ground. The horse bolts, galloping toward Edinburgh with its sole occupant: "the body of the dead and long-dissected Gray."

The affairs of Burke, Hare and Knox are history at the outset of "The Body-Snatcher." By using Fettes' story as a vehicle, Stevenson provides the reader with thinly disguised, historically accurate information about the anatomist:

> There was, at that period, a certain extramural teacher of anatomy, whom I shall designate by the letter K. His

name was subsequently too well known. The man who bore it skulked through the streets of Edinburgh in disguise, while the mob that applauded at the execution of Burke called loudly for the blood of his employer. But Mr. K--- was then at the top of his vogue; he enjoyed a popularity due partly to his own talent and address, partly to the incapacity of his rival, the university professor. The students, at least, swore by his name, and Fettes believed himself, and was believed by others, to have laid the foundations of success when he had acquired the favour of this meteorically famous man.

Prior to the mention of Fettes, this passage, with its obvious references to Robert Knox, could be included in an encyclopedia entry on the Burke and Hare murders. The "university professor" he mentions is Alexander Monro. Another of his references to Burke and Hare occurs a few pages later, when Fettes hears "grumbling Irish voices" emanating from the men who have brought him the corpse of Jane Galbraith, the well-known street singer. Stevenson based his Gray, the "resurrection man," on James Gray, the witness who testified against Burke at the trial, and Fettes on Knox's assistant, David Paterson.

Like Stevenson's earlier "The Sire de Maletroit's Door," "The Body-Snatcher" weaves history with fictional characters and somewhat fantastical events; and the Edinburgh and Pentland Hills locations lend an authentic atmosphere to the gruesome proceedings. Similar in structure to "Maletroit," the narrative moves at a brisk pace and is highlighted by descriptive and poetical prose. When Macfarlane eludes Fettes at the George, Stevenson provides vivid imagery: "He crouched together, brushing on the wainscot, and made a dart like a serpent, striking for the door."

Rather than attempting to write "objective" history, Stevenson incorporated aspects of the past into his creative fiction, using factual events in Scotland as a springboard for his characterizations and storylines. As he used the Burke and Hare murders in "The Body-Snatcher," he later drew on pirate lore for *Treasure Island* and the 1745 Jacobite Rebellion and its aftermath for *Kidnapped*, *The Master of Ballantrae* (1889) and *Catriona* (1893).

In his 1884 essay "A Humble Remonstrance," a rejoinder to Henry James' "The Art of Fiction," Stevenson writes, "What then is the object, what the method, of an art, and what the source of its power? The whole secret is that no art 'does compete with life.' Man's one method, whether he reasons or creates, is to half-shut his eyes against the confusion of reality."

Late in August 1881, Stevenson conceived "The Sea Cook: A Story for Boys" in a rented Highland cottage at Braemar. Again troubled by wet, windy weather, he remained indoors, joining Lloyd to experiment with a box of paints, passing the time by sketching the map of an "imaginary island."

Completing 15 chapters in as many days, Louis was motivated by illness and, after leaving Scotland, continued working on the first draft at Weybridge in Surrey, and during a two-week session at his winter home in Davos, Switzerland. Lloyd had inspired him to write a boys' adventure story, but an additional impetus was provided by his father, who discussed various points of the tale and suggested the scene of Jim Hawkins in the apple barrel, the specific contents of Captain Billy Bones' sea chest, and the name *Walrus* for Captain Flint's old ship.[12] In a July 1884 letter to his friend Sidney Colvin, Louis revealed, "'Treasure Island' came out of Kingsley's 'At Last,' where I got the Dead Man's Chest—and that was the seed—and out of the great Captain Johnson's 'History of the Great Pirates.'"[13]

One month after Louis and Lloyd's brainstorm instigated by children's paints, the first chapters of "The Sea Cook" began to be published in *Young Folks* magazine. Eventually the entire novel ran in 17 weekly installments from October 1, 1881, through January 28, 1882. Stevenson declined to use his real name and titled the serialized novel "Treasure Island; or, The Mutiny of the Hispaniola. By Captain George North." (On November 15, 1883, Cassell and Company published the novel as *Treasure Island*, and Boston's Roberts Brothers released the U.S. edition three months later.)

During the spring of 1882, Dr. Karl Ruedi suggested that Louis seek permanent residence in the south of France, "fifteen miles from the sea and near a pine forest."[14] The high altitude of the Swiss Alps was no longer required for his slowly improving condition; but, rather than accepting the physician's prescription, he followed the advice of his parents, who longed to see him back in Scotland.

Robert Louis Stevenson, Davos, Switzerland, 1882.

For the remainder of the year, he sought lodgings in London, Edinburgh and the Scottish countryside. Although he should have known better, his exposure to the cool, damp climate worsened his condition and he began haemorrhaging again. As biographer James Pope Hennesy points out, "most of the good of the long months under Dr. Ruedi's intelligent care at Davos was undone."[15]

Completed in April 1882, "The Silverado Squatters: Sketches from a California Mountain," documenting the Stevensons' California honeymoon during June-July 1880, eventually appeared in two installments in the November and December 1883 issues of *Century Illustrated Monthly Magazine*. (First published in book form by Chatto and Windus on January 8, 1884, *The Silverado Squatters* appeared in a U.S. edition, released by Roberts Brothers, later that month.)

The Stevensons returned to France in September 1882 and briefly lived at Campagne Defli, St. Marcel, a suburb of Marseilles. Fanny, fearing a breakout of typhus, sent Louis to Nice while she packed their belongings. Several days later, railway officials told her that the ailing Louis probably had died, but she eventually found him lounging in a Nice hotel. In March 1883, they began a nine-month residence at La Solitude, a chalet at Hyeres, but the change of climate did nothing to improve Louis' rapidly worsening condition.

Another near-fatal haemorrhage rendered his right arm useless as he spent several days propped up in bed, writing portions of *A Child's Garden of Verses* with his left hand. He later developed sciatica (a neuralgia of the sensory and motor nerve that runs through the pelvis and upper leg) and Egyptian ophthalmia, a malady that quickly spread throughout the village. Able to leave his bed for only short periods of time, he worked on the manuscripts for two novels, "The Black Arrow: A Tale of Tunstall Forest," a romantic tale set during the Wars of the Roses, commissioned by *Young Folks* editor James Henderson, and *Prince Otto*.

(After beginning its 17-week run in *Young Folks* on June 30, 1883 [again under the *nom de plume* "Captain George North"], *The Black Arrow: A Tale of the Two Roses* was published in book form by Charles Scribner's Sons in 1888. Ostensibly completed by December 1883, *Prince Otto*, first serialized as seven monthly installments [April-October 1885] in *Longman's Magazine*, was published in book form, as *Prince Otto: A Romance*, by Chatto and Windus.)

Following brief stays at Vichy, Clermont-Ferrand, and Royat during the spring and summer of 1883, the Stevensons returned to Hyeres. In January 1884, they joined W. E. Henley and Charles Baxter in Nice, where Louis became so ill that he could not speak without spilling blood onto his clothes. From Hyeres they again travelled to Royat and, during the summer, moved to Bournemouth on the west cliff in southern England. "The Body-Snatcher" finally entered the public scene when the *Pall Mall Christmas Extra* hit the streets in December.

Stevenson was a brilliant stylist, but he did not believe that beautiful prose was the *sine qua non* of literature. In a letter to Henry James written at the time "The Body-Snatcher" was published, he explained,

> People suppose it is the "stuff" that interests them; they think, for instance, that the prodigious fine thoughts and sentiments in Shakespeare impress by their own weight, not understanding that the unpolished diamond is but a stone. They think that striking situations, or good dialogue, are got by studying life; they will not rise to understand that they are prepared by deliberate artifice and set off by painful suppressions.[16]

In "A Humble Remonstrance," his riposte to James, published in the December 1884 *Longman's Magazine*, he argued,

> From all its chapters, from all its pages, from all its sentences, the well-written novel echoes and re-echoes its one creative and controlling thought: to this must every incident and character contribute; the style must have been pitched in unison with this; and if there is anywhere a word that looks another way, the book would be stronger, clearer, and (I had almost said) fuller without it.

Shortly after *A Child's Garden of Verses* was published in March 1885, Louis and his family moved into "Skerryvore," a home Louis named after Uncle Alan Stevenson's lighthouse located west of the Isle of Mull

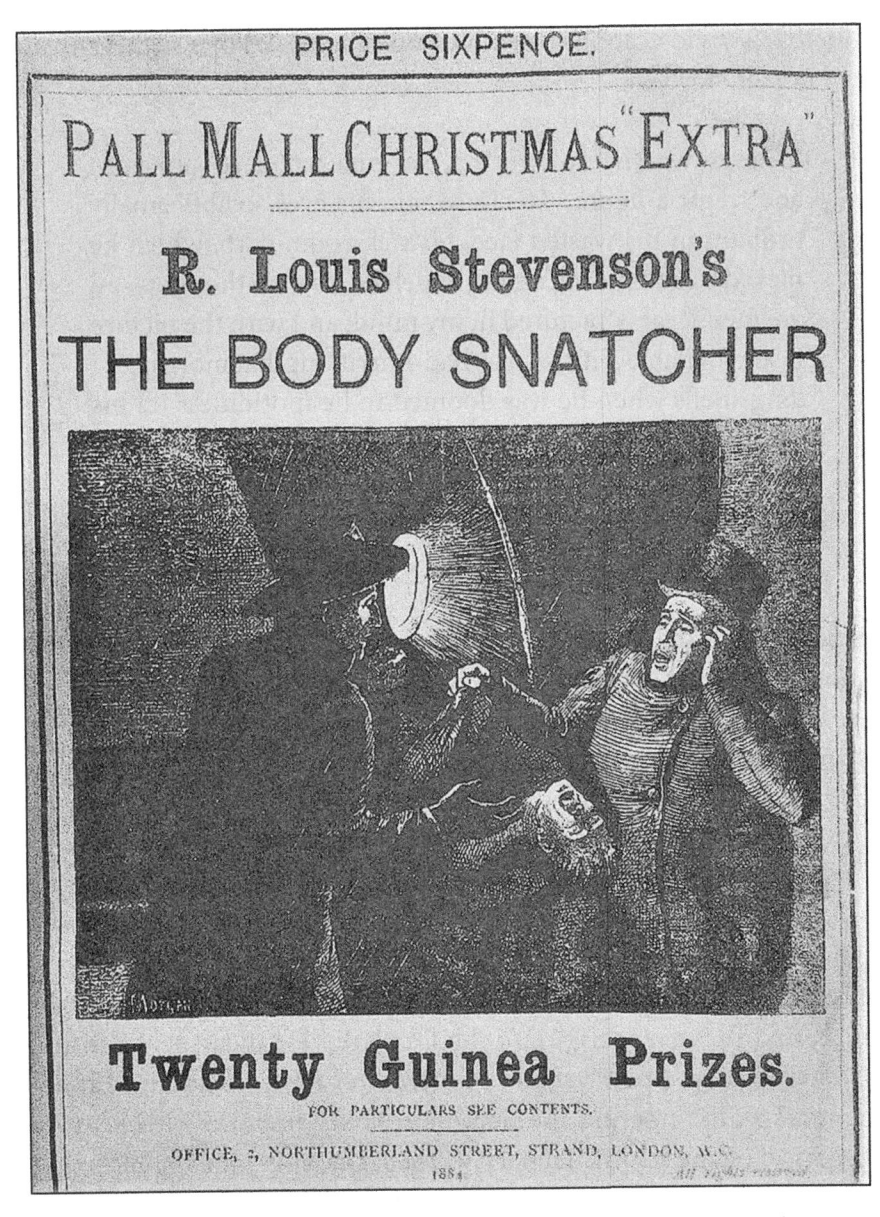

"The Body-Snatcher," published in *The Pall Mall Christmas Extra*, December 1884.

on Dhu Heartach. In return for her cooperation in Thomas' effort to keep Louis in Great Britain, Fanny received the house as a belated wedding gift. Lloyd Osbourne described Skerryvore as "unusually attractive," but claimed that it was a virtual prison for his invalid stepfather. His vivid account resembles a passage from one of Stevenson's own horror stories:

> [N]ever was he so spectral, so emaciated, so unkempt and tragic a figure. His long hair, his eyes so abnormally brilliant in his wasted face, his sick-room garb, which he picked up at random and to which he gave no thought—all are ineffaceably pictured in my mind; and with the picture is an ineffable pity.... He had horrifying haemorrhages; long spells when he was doomed to lie motionless on his bed lest the slightest movement would re-start the flow; when he would speak in whispers, and one sat beside him and tried to be entertaining—in the room he was only too likely to leave in his coffin.[17]

Although he suffered terribly during his two-year residence at Skerryvore, Stevenson wrote some of his best and most influential works. *The Strange Case of Dr. Jekyll and Mr. Hyde* and *Kidnapped*, stories that established his international reputation, were both penned while he sought refuge from England's cool, damp climate.

During an evening's sleep in September 1885, Louis dreamed "a fine bogy tale," which he began documenting at the crack of dawn. A few days later, he read the results to Lloyd and Fanny, who dismissed it as a work of lurid horror. After venting his rage, Louis returned to his bedroom, but soon descended the stairs, admitted she was right, and tossed the manuscript into the fireplace. He then spent the next six days writing a new version of *Jekyll and Hyde*, including Fanny's suggestion of tempering the dual-personality premise with a strong allegorical element. On January 9, 1886, the novel was published by London's Longmans, Green and Company, four days after Charles Scribner's Sons distributed the U.S. version.

Much speculation has been offered about Stevenson's inspiration for the dual personality, noting the influence of his strict Calvinist upbringing, his use of various prescribed drugs, and the effects of his lifelong illnesses. Prior to writing the story, he had witnessed his distinguished friend Walter Ferrier succumb to alcoholism, and he also was familiar with Edinburgh cabinet-maker Deacon Brodie (1741-1788),

Robert Louis Stevenson, Skerryvore, Bournemouth, 1885.

who had been hanged for leading a double life. Brodie, who specialized in robbing respectable citizens' homes after inviting them to parties, had provided the raw material for Stevenson and W. E. Henley's 1880 play, *Deacon Brodie*.

Stevenson's realization of the dual personality predated similar theories advanced by European psychologists. More than seven years after *Jekyll and Hyde* became a public sensation, Sigmund Freud and Joseph Breuer published their first paper on hysteria. In *The Definitive Dr. Jekyll and Mr. Hyde Companion*, Harry M. Geduld notes, "In this and the papers that followed, Freud examined the reasons why hysterics split off pieces of consciousness and forgot them: the pieces contain painful or socially unacceptable or infantile ideas and wishes." In the novel, Stevenson anticipated Freud by allowing Hyde to represent the unacceptable ideas of Jekyll.[18]

In November 1884, nearly a year before experiencing the nightmare that became *Jekyll and Hyde*, Stevenson had written "Markheim," an eerie allegory about a criminal's guilty conscience, indicating that he was moving beyond the more straightforward approach he established with earlier "crawlers" (as he called them) like "Thrawn Janet," "The Body-Snatcher" and "The Merry Men." One month after completing *Jekyll and Hyde*, he wrote "Ollala," a haunting tale of horror, beauty, love and sadness, reminiscent of Edgar Allan Poe's "The Fall of the House of Usher." (Stevenson's subsequent horror-fantasy stories include the South Seas tales "The Bottle Imp" and "The Isle of Voices," involving a hellish genie and a wizard, respectively; and the posthumously published "The Waif Woman," set in Iceland and featuring a vengeful corpse. All three are fantastic fables in which materialism is conquered by supernatural forces.)

At Skerryvore, Louis also indulged his love of Celtic music, and the poetry and songwriting of Robert Burns in part influenced his interest in traditional Scottish songs, particularly those written during or shortly after the 1745 Jacobite Rebellion. Jenni Calder explains,

> Music continued to absorb him, but that would never be a success. He sent his efforts at composition to Bob [Stevenson] for comment. He and Lloyd—"You should hear Lloyd on the penny whistle, and me on the piano! Dear powers, what a concerto!"—were sending their neighbors, he alleged, "in quest of brighter climes!" It was all part of the need for expression.[19]

Other than the piano, Louis' favorite instruments included the tin whistle and the a cappella voice, as many of his novelistic passages demonstrate, and the flageolet, a small fipple flute that he liked to play while sitting in bed.

Kidnapped, like "The Body-Snatcher" before it, was inspired by actual events in Scotland's history, specifically the Appin Murder of 1752. In *The Scenery of Dreams*, Lachlan Munro explains the impetus for Stevenson to write his greatest historical adventure:

> The aftermath of the Jacobite Rebellion in 1745 has been fruitful for Scottish novelists and historians. The romantic and hopeless loyalty of the defeated clansmen, the invention of a folk tradition and the writing of the finest "folk" songs in Europe, the final vanishing of Scotland's independence and most distinctive and picturesque way of life, which developed into the nostalgic emotions of "The Lost Cause." All these combined to give the Jacobites a central place in Scottish sentiment, even among Saxon-achs like Scott and Stevenson, who, despite their Toryism, sprang from the Protestant Whig tradition.[20]

Henry James considered *Kidnapped* to be Stevenson's finest book. Louis, too, would name it the favorite of his own novels.

In May 1887, life at Skerryvore was interrupted by news of Thomas Stevenson's rapidly deteriorating health. Louis rushed to Edinburgh, and Fanny was shocked when his father failed to recognize him. Disgusted at the prospect of dying in bed, Thomas wished to be attired properly while smoking his beloved pipe. A private funeral was scheduled but became "the largest such…occasion that Edinburgh had ever seen." Having caught a serious cold, Louis was barred from the cemetery by his uncle, Dr. George Balfour. Rather than mourning at the graveside, he paid his respects by completing "Ticonderoga," a ballad he recently had discussed with Thomas.

A few months after he returned to Skerryvore, Stevenson's doctors advised him that he could no longer reside in Great Britain without risking further, perhaps fatal, illnesses. He considered a resort for consumptives in Colorado; and, accompanied by Fanny, Lloyd, Margaret, and his nurse, Valentine Roch, sailed from London aboard the *Ludgate Hill* on August 22, 1887.

From that moment, when he did adieu to his native land, until December 3, 1894, his last day at Vailima, Upolu, Samoa, his vagabond lifestyle, intended to improve his precarious health, took him far and wide. A cold winter at Saranac Lake in the New York Adirondacks (where he began writing *The Master of Ballantrae*), was followed by a return to California and a Pacific voyage aboard the 95-foot schooner *Casco* to the Marquesas Islands, Fakarava Atoll, Tahiti and Hawaii. In Honolulu, he completed *Ballantrae* and *The Wrong Box* (a collaboration with Lloyd), as well as enjoying lengthy "champagne parties" with King Kalakaua). He also took a week-long jaunt to the leper colony on Molokai (inspiring his 1890 defense of recently deceased Belgian missionary Father Damien de Veuster, "Father Damien: An Open Letter to the Reverend Hyde of Honolulu"). During a cruise through Micronesia aboard the *Equator*, a San Francisco-based trading schooner, he

Aboard the schooner *Casco*: Fanny Stevenson, King Kalakaua, Margaret Stevenson, Lloyd Osbourne, Robert Louis Stevenson, Captain O.H. Otis, Hawaii, 1889.

and Lloyd co-wrote another novel, *The Wrecker*, a maritime detective tale based on actual incidents.

After a six-week stay at Butaritari in the Gilbert Islands, the *Equator* docked at Apemama, where the party was stranded for two months while Captain Reid and his crew sailed off to gather copra. Threading its way through the remainder of the Gilbert atolls, the schooner braved a terrible storm before docking at Upolu on December 7, 1889. Intent on collecting additional information for his book *In the South Seas*, Stevenson planned to stay for two months before returning to England, but he quickly grew attached to the location.

A few weeks after their arrival, Louis purchased 400 acres of land above the town of Apia and ordered a new home to be built. Except for a cruise aboard the *Janet Nichol* to the Gilbert, Marshall and New Caledonian Islands from April to August 1890, and a few excursions to Sydney, the Stevensons remained in Samoa. The Vailima estate eventually housed his stepdaughter, Isobel, her husband, Joe Strong, and son, Austin, plus Lloyd, Margaret, and seven Samoan aides, some of whom, on ceremonial occasions, donned the "official uniform" created by Louis: a loincloth of Royal Stewart tartan![21]

At Vailima, Stevenson finished *Catriona*, his sequel to *Kidnapped*, *The Ebb-Tide*, and several short stories. He also began two complex novels, *Weir of Hermiston* and *St. Ives*. Originally titled "The Justice Clerk," *Weir* includes a brilliant vision of Scotland conjured up amid his new Samoan surroundings. Considered by many to be his finest work, this (destined to be unfinished) novel fell by the wayside when he turned to *St. Ives*, but he occasionally did revert to the earlier effort. Having suffered a severe attack of writer's cramp during the summer of 1892, Louis began dictating his work to Isobel. The Samoan weather allowed him a respite from the respiratory problems which had plagued him in Europe and the United States, but his health continued to deteriorate. The thematics of his fiction became more somber, as did his correspondence with trusted friends.

On August 23, 1893, Louis wrote to Sidney Colvin:

> Life is not all Beer and Skittles; and mine is closing in dark enough. What is left, my God, in such a welter? When does blame come in? Nowhere, I believe, or very little.

Only the inherent tragedy of things works itself out from white to black and blacker, and the poor things of a day look ruefully on.[22]

During the late afternoon of his final day, while taking a break from dictating *Weir of Hermiston* to Isobel, Louis decided to help Fanny in the kitchen. Fetching a bottle of burgundy from the cellar, he added cooking oil to a mayonnaise that she was preparing for dinner. After walking onto the veranda, he spoke, suddenly clasped his hands to his head, and cried out excitedly. (Various accounts claim that he uttered, "Oh, my head!" "What's that?" or "What a pain!") Turning to Fanny, he painfully asked, "Do I look strange?"

Fanny grabbed one of Louis' arms and, aided by their valet Sosimo, guided him into an armchair in the hall. Losing consciousness, Louis never recovered and, though his doctor arrived a short time later, he died from a cerebral haemorrhage at 8:10 p.m., aged 44 years, three weeks.

The burial of Robert Louis Stevenson atop Mount Vaea: Lloyd Osbourne is at right, Apia, Upolu, Samoa, December 1894.

Samoan natives at the grave of Robert Louis Stevenson, after completion of the monument, mid-1890s.

Stevenson's death shocked admirers throughout the world, but perhaps his Samoan friends were affected to the greatest extent. Many natives took part in his unconventional funeral service. Lloyd acquired necessary tools in Apia and sent messages to several island chiefs who, together with their workers, cleared a path to the summit of Mount Vaea, the spot Louis had chosen as his final resting place. About 50 strong Samoan men took turns carrying the casket up the steep mountainside, while Fanny, Isobel and Margaret watched from the veranda of Vailima.

Sixty natives and 19 European friends attended the service, including a reading by the Reverend Clarke, a British missionary, and a brief eulogy in Samoan by the Reverend Newell. After the mourners made their way back down the mountain, an aged Samoan chief turned toward the grave, adding, "*Tofa, Tusitala. Tofa, Tusitala*" ["Sleep, Teller of Tales"].

Later, a stone memorial, resembling a Samoan chief's monument, was erected upon the sepulchre. Included in the engravings are a thistle and hibiscus flower (the national emblems of Scotland and Samoa, respectively), a tiger lily (representing the independence of Fanny Stevenson, whose ashes were buried there a year after her death on February 18, 1914), and both verses of Stevenson's "Requiem."

Although purely coincidental, the monument ensured that Stevenson's earthly remains reposed in an impenetrable tomb, a far cry from the temporary resting places of the early 19th-century Edinburgh unfortunates whose fates echo hauntingly through his unforgettable story, "The Body-Snatcher," and the subsequent motion picture adapted from it.

3
The Body Snatcher:
The Val Lewton Production

DURING THE EARLY 1940S, while Universal Pictures was turning out formulaic imitations of its successful horror films of the early to mid-1930s, Val Lewton and his low-budget team at RKO Radio created a new type of screen terror, a style relying on suggestive, eerie visuals and sound effects, understated acting, and spare, literate writing, rather than a straightforward depiction of supernatural monsters and physical action. Lewton, who referred to his films as psychological or historical thrillers, researched each of them extensively, often incorporating actual events into the narratives.

Born Vladimir Ivan Leventon in Yalta, Russia, on May 7, 1904, Lewton emigrated to the United States in 1911 and was educated at Columbia University. A member of a prestigious family, he was the son of Yakov Leventon, a chemist who reportedly served Tsar Alexander III, and the nephew of celebrated actress Alla Nazimova [Adelaide Leventon].

Lewton's ability to adapt literary material for the screen was considerable. Prior to 1933, when he began working as a story editor for David O. Selznick, he wrote and published nine novels, six nonfiction works, a collection of poetry, and *Jasmine*, a pornographic book. He and future collaborator Jacques Tourneur arranged "revolutionary scenes" for Metro-Goldwyn-Mayer's *A Tale of Two Cities* (1935), directed by Jack Conway (with uncredited help from Robert Z. Leonard). In May 1936, he was the first person at Selznick International to read Margaret Mitchell's then unfinished *Gone with the Wind*, which he summarized for the producer, calling the lengthy story "ponderous trash."[1]

In 1942, RKO created the low-budget horror unit. Charles Koerner, the studio's executive vice president, chose Lewton as its creative force, dictating that the unit produce horror "programmers" to cost no more than $150,000 each and run no longer than 75 minutes. Though he was limited by these restrictions, Lewton and his associates created some of the most thoughtful and artistically powerful "horror" films of the 1940s or any other decade.

Quite different from what audiences expected, the successful *Cat People* (1942) initiated a series including *I Walked with a Zombie* (1943), *The Leopard Man* (1943), *The Seventh Victim* (1943), *The Ghost Ship* (1943), *The Curse of the Cat People* (1944), *The Body Snatcher* (1945), *Isle of the Dead* (1945) and *Bedlam* (1946). Koerner crafted the lurid titles, which often are unrepresentative of the subtle style and psychological content Lewton and his collaborators invested in the films. The "horror" frequently results from the effects mortality elicits from the human psyche.

Throughout the Lewton series, characters become trapped by an aspect of the everyday world, usually when merely attempting to survive from one day to the next: a young woman seeking affection in *Cat People* or walking to the market to obtain some food in *The Leopard Man*. Lewton chose not to set his productions within a supernatural context, but instead stressed terror existing in the natural world.

Lewton's thematics are visually sustained with a claustrophobic style of cinematography and editing, often placing the characters (and audience) in an uncomfortable position. Depth is added to this visual strategy through the exploration of legends and historical events, helping to situate the stories within a believable context.

Lewton's debut as a producer was impressive in a 1940s film industry permeated with mandated wartime propaganda, conventionality and the strictures imposed by the Production Code of 1934. The subtlety and intelligence of *Cat People* was praised by many, including

Lewton's former employer, who wired his enthusiasm on December 14, 1942:

> Dear Val:
> I saw *Cat People* last night, and I am very proud of you. I think it is an altogether superb producing job, and is in every way a much better picture than ninety percent of the "A" product that I have seen in recent months.....Indeed, I think it is one of the most credible and skillfully worked out horror pieces in many years.....I am sending a copy of this wire by mail to Mr. Koerner, who I am sure feels as I do, that RKO is fortunate to have made such a ten strike as the acquisition of your services as a producer. Other studios hopefully have extended such opportunities to would-be producers by the score without getting a result such as you have delivered at the outset.
> Sincerely,
> David O. Selznick[2]

The Body Snatcher is the only Lewton series film based on a classic literary work. RKO executive producer Jack Gross, interested in signing Boris Karloff to a contract, suggested that Lewton cast the star in one of his fright films. Robert Wise, who had replaced Gunther Fritsch as director on *The Curse of the Cat People* and then helmed *Mademoiselle Fifi* (1944) for the producer, recalled, "Lewton, with nothing personal against Mr. Karloff, found this not much to his taste, but searched for story material that would have quality, even though he was using the 'scare' actor who had made his name as Frankenstein's Monster."[3]

Karloff agreed to meet Lewton at the studio, where they were joined by Wise and Mark Robson. Having returned to making formula horror pictures at Universal following the major Broadway and touring success of *Arsenic and Old Lace* (1941-1944), Karloff was anxious to appear in a quality cinematic project. He immediately found Lewton and his cohorts a fine fit, and the feeling was mutual. Wise said,

> It was strange—the first meeting....I had never seen [Karloff] except on the screen—and this was before [he made a] color film. When he first walked in the door I was startled by his coloring, the strange bluish cast—but when he turned those eyes on us, and that velvet voice said, "Good afternoon, gentlemen," we were his, and never thought about anything else.[4]

Lewton searched for story material including characters suited to Karloff's talents. He initially chose for inspiration, not a literary work, but an artistic one: the 1883 Arnold Böcklin painting "Isle of the Dead." Turning to the tales of Stevenson, he then discovered the character of Gray in "The Body-Snatcher" and realized that he could enlarge the role and other aspects of the story. In a May 10, 1944, RKO interdepartment communication to Jack Gross, Lewton wrote,

> Subject to your approval, we have decided upon Robert Louis Stevenson's "The Body-Snatcher" as the best possible subject for the second Karloff picture. The story needs development because as it is told now, the character we would like Karloff to play is a fragmentary one called "Gray." But if you will read the story you will see the possibility of developing Gray into a truly horrendous person.
>
> You probably want to know the reasons for our selection of this story above the others. They are as follows:
>
> 1. The title seems good to us.
> 2. There is exploitation value in the use of a famous Robert Louis Stevenson classic.
> 3. There is ninety percent chance that this is in the public domain. The legal department is now searching the title.
> 4. The characters are colorful. The background of London [sic] medical life in the 1830s is extremely interesting. The sets are limited in number but effective in type. The costumes are readily procurable and no great difficulties of any sort so far as production is concerned are evident.

5. There is also an excellent part for Bela Lugosi as a resurrection man.[5]

On February 5, 1944, the radio program *Inner Sanctum* had broadcast the episode "Dealer in Death," starring Laird Cregar as Hare. The actor was in New York, making personal appearances to promote his performance as Jack the Ripper in the 20th Century-Fox thriller *The Lodger* (1944), directed by John Brahm, and soon would play a similar role in *Hangover Square* (1945) for the same studio and director. In *Bela Lugosi and Boris Karloff*, Gregory Mank notes,

> It's possible Lewton had heard the broadcast, or heard of it. To publicize the show, Cregar and company had gotten into costume, gone to Gimbel's Manhattan department store's antique shop (that doubled as a 19th century inn), and posed for pictures—winning the episode a three-page spread in the February 7, 1944, edition of *Life* magazine.[6]

On May 18, 1944, Karloff, approving both of Lewton's story proposals, and guaranteed $6,000 weekly on each picture, signed the RKO "star" contract. Six weeks later, on August 1, *Motion Picture Daily* announced that the actor was working on "'The Isle of the Dead' [and] will be seen on Broadway next winter in the starring role in Hulber Footner's 'Who Sups with the Devil,'" for which he reportedly had been signed by the *Arsenic and Old Lace* team of Howard Lindsay and Russell Crouse.[7]

Contrary to the trade paper's account, *Isle of the Dead* had been suspended on July 24, when Karloff underwent spinal surgery for an "acute arthritic condition" at Good Samaritan Hospital. Requiring a month-long hospitalization, his recuperation forced RKO to reschedule *Isle of the Dead* for early December, freeing Lewton to focus on *The Body Snatcher*. (Moreover, the Footner play became another in a string of proposed Karloff projects that was not produced.)

While Karloff recovered from his own bit of surgical "horror," and Lewton developed ideas for his next excursion into the cinematic variety, the Home Army of the Polish underground resistance began its Uprising in Warsaw, which had been under Nazi occupation for nearly five years. The attempt to liberate the city was timed to coincide with the retreat of the Germans from approaching Soviet forces. The operation began on August 1 and would last 63 days, marking the largest military effort undertaken by a European resistance movement during World War II. Provided no support by Russia, the Poles received supplies dropped by the RAF (in 200 low-level operations) after Winston Churchill skirted Soviet authorization. The U.S. Army Air Forces also completed one high-level drop after Soviet air clearance was granted. The Uprising finally was quashed, and Warsaw subsequently destroyed, by the Germans after the Red Army's decision to halt upon reaching the eastern outskirts of the city allowed them to regroup. Polish military casualties greatly outnumbered those of the Germans, with the massacres of Polish civilians reaching an appalling figure (estimated from 150,000 to 200,000).

Meanwhile, back in Hollywood, where a censorial institution soon would accuse the Russian-born Lewton of producing "excessive gruesomeness" with his atmospheric shadow plays, he worked on the screenplay for *The Body Snatcher*. Adopting the pseudonym "Carlos Keith," he collaborated with Philip MacDonald, author of the novel *Patrol* (which twice was adapted for the cinema, most recently for RKO's *The Lost Patrol* [1934], directed by John Ford and co-starring Karloff). His first six choices for a writing partner, including Michael Hogan (*King Solomon's Mines* [1937], *Rebecca* [1940]), had been rejected as too expensive by Gross, whom Lewton referred to as "an abysmally ignorant and stupid man" in an August 24, 1944, letter to his mother and sister.[8] His selection of Wise as director, however, faced no such resistance.

Lewton, partly due to budget constraints, eliminated the opening section of Stevenson's story, in which the aged Fettes meets Macfarlane at the George, instead choosing to begin the narrative in 1831, two years after the affairs of Burke, Hare and Knox. The character of "Toddy" MacFarlane (the "f" is capitalized in the film version) replaces Dr. K--- as head of the anatomy school and Fettes is appointed as his lab assistant. Well-researched, the script assigns many of the historical Robert Knox's qualities to MacFarlane, while Fettes' characterization is enlarged from the original. Knox is referred to by name, but has fled to London, leaving MacFarlane in power. Although the character roles are altered in the film, many of Stevenson's passages are included in expanded form.

Early drafts prepared by MacDonald transformed Gray into the full-fledged "resurrection man" who uses his previous "shielding" of MacFarlane during Burke's trial to blackmail the doctor. During the story conferences, when Gross requested that graphic material be added to the proceedings, Lewton inserted a scene into the treatment, in which Mrs. MacBride (eventually played by Mary Gordon) "passes through the horrors of attempting to identify her dead son among the flotsam and jetsam of human limbs and portions on the anatomy tables."[9]

On September 11, Lewton wrote to Ben Piazza of the RKO casting office:

> Gray, the cabman, although in point of footage subservient to MacFarlane… is the most important part and so far Boris Karloff, who is to play it (God willing) agrees on the value of the character… Josef [sic], the janitor, is a sneak; servile and consumed with evil cunning. The character of Josef should present us with few difficulties as far as casting is concerned.[10]

Lewton did encounter a difficulty, however, in the form of censorship waged by the Production Code Administration, whose representative sent him a missive on September 27:

> We have read with close attention your estimating script of September 8, for your proposed picture *Body Snatcher*, and regret to advise that this story is unacceptable under the provisions of the code. Because of the repellent nature of such matter, which has to do with graverobbing, dissecting bodies, and pickling bodies…[11]

In *Bela Lugosi and Boris Karloff*, Gregory Mank perceptively describes Lewton's probable state of mind at this juncture:

> The Breen Office's red light scuttling of *The Body Snatcher* had a two-fold effect on the producer. Naturally, the hypersensitive Lewton despaired. Jack Gross had demanded gore,

and now the Breen Office demanded the gore removed. Yet, for an irreverent soul like Lewton, the Breen Office's shock over the material only made Lewton all the more hell-bent on making the movie. Vowing to save his new horror show, Lewton personally went back to work on the script. Since Breen counseled that the film's only hope was "some new locales, away from dead bodies, and new dialogue situations," Lewton developed further the romance between young medical student Fettes and the Widow Marsh (adding a bit of relief to the tale), cut Mrs. MacBride's horrific trip to the anatomy room, and eventually—as was his custom—wrote all of the final screenplay himself. Philip MacDonald, fearful the film might flop, demanded Lewton share the blame if indeed it did. Hence Lewton took screenplay credit (under the *nom de plume* of "Carlos Keith").[12]

Another element that concerned the PCA was the depiction of "burking." Ultimately, however, Gray's use of the term "burke" and murderous implementation of the method were filmed and used in the final cut.

Several new characters are featured in the film, including four females: Meg Cameron, MacFarlane's "secret" bride; Mrs. Marsh, a young widow; her injured daughter, Georgina, who is confined to a wheelchair; and Mrs. McBride. Many of Stevenson's stories lack visible female characters, but he did not ignore women out of prejudice or indifference, as some critics have charged. The scarcity of women in his early stories may be attributed to several factors: the dearth of realistic sexual elements in Victorian popular fiction, the traditional absence of females in the adventure genre, the male-dominated historical eras in which the tales are set, and the audience for whom he was writing. The stories first appeared in periodicals and boys' adventure magazines that were read predominantly by males. During the mid- to late-1880s, his readership expanded, and, as his literary talent continued to evolve, stronger and more interesting women began to appear.

But, even as late as 1892, when an editor sought to expurgate "The Beach of Falesa," his attempts at female characterization were constricted by Victorian prudishness. On January 31 of that year, Louis wrote to Sidney Colvin, "This is a poison-bad world for the romancer,

Boris Karloff publicity portrait used by RKO Radio to publicize *The Body Snatcher*.

this Anglo-Saxon world; I usually get out of it by not having any women in it at all; but when I remember I had 'The Treasure of Franchard' refused as unfit for a family magazine, I feel despair weigh upon my wrists."[13]

Affected by the dictates of the PCA's Joseph Breen that the screenplay for *The Body Snatcher* include "some new locales, away from dead bodies, and new dialogue situations," Lewton expanded the romantic subplot involving Fettes and Mrs. Marsh. In fact, Hollywood screenwriters invariably added women and romantic subplots to Stevenson's stories, most famously in the sexualizing of *The Strange Case of Dr. Jekyll and Mr. Hyde*, a tale devoid of major female characters. Only four women are mentioned in the novella: a maidservant, a match girl, and the doctor's housemaid and cook. Adapted by Thomas Russell Sullivan for actor Richard Mansfield, the 1887 play *Dr. Jekyll and Mr. Hyde* is the source of the major female characters who would be integrated, with variations, into most subsequent stage and film dramatizations.

The one prominent additional male character in *The Body Snatcher* is the servant Joseph, whose name recalls that of a real-life Burke and Hare murder victim. But Lewton's most significant improvement on Stevenson's characters is the enlargement of Gray (here called "John Gray, Cabman"). Though the "resurrection man" appears only briefly, but memorably, in a few paragraphs of the story, the presence of his cinematic counterpart is felt continually, both on- and off-screen.

In his second directorial assignment, Wise appreciated the fact that Karloff, regardless of circumstances, never held up production:

> Karloff was not particularly well at the time. He was having a lot of back problems, but he didn't let that stop him at all. He was in there working as hard and as steady and as strong as he could.... seriously, he never complained... he just gritted his teeth and did it. And one of my best experiences—he was quite a different man than he appeared on the screen. He was very well educated, a very sensitive man, a very tasteful man.... He was a very, very, very lovely person—very warm and very kind. We got to be quite friendly for a period of time....[14]

On Wednesday, October 25, 1944, *Motion Picture Daily* announced, "Bela Lugosi has been added to the cast of RKO's 'The Body Snatcher,' which stars Boris Karloff."[15] Appearing opposite Karloff for the eighth time, Lugosi had been worked successfully into the script by Lewton,

RKO Radio publicity portrait of Bela Lugosi as Joseph.

not as a "resurrection man," but still providing the actor with his first quality role in many years. Gross reportedly had suggested that Lewton cast him as "Toddy" MacFarlane, but Wise later confirmed, "The whole part of Joseph actually was created to accommodate the casting of Lugosi....We never considered giving Lugosi the role of MacFarlane. He didn't have the right quality for it...."[16]

Rita Corday as Mrs. Marsh and Henry Daniell as Dr. MacFarlane.

Prior to the casting of Henry Daniell, several actors' names were mentioned for the MacFarlane role, including Albert Dekker, John Emery (who had just played Jean Cornudet in *Mademoiselle Fifi*), George Coulouris, Philip Merivale and Alan Napier (who worked in *Cat People* and *Mademoiselle Fifi*). Before Daniell was set, head-to-head, against Karloff, he impressively had supported Greta Garbo in *Camille*, Jeanette MacDonald in *The Firefly* and Gladys George in *Madame X* (all 1937), Norma Shearer in *Marie Antoinette* (1938), Katharine Hepburn in *Holiday* (1938) and *The Philadelphia Story* (1940), Paul Muni in *We Are Not Alone* (1939), Errol Flynn in *The Private Lives of Elizabeth and Essex* (1939) and *The Sea Hawk* (1940), and Charles Chaplin in *Great Dictator* (1940), giving one of his most memorable performances, as "Herr Garbitsch," his lampoon on Josef Goebbels, opposite the director-star's "Adenoid Hynkel, Dictator of Tomania." More recently, he had appeared in popular detective series films, opposite Sidney Toler's Charlie Chan (*Castle in the Desert* [1942]) and Basil Rathbone's Sherlock Holmes (*Sherlock Holmes and the Voice of Terror* [1942] and *Sherlock Holmes in Washington* [1943]). He also played Henry Brocklehurst in Aldous Huxley's adaptation of Charlotte Bronte's *Jane Eyre* (1943), directed by Robert Stevenson and co-starring Orson Welles and Joan Fontaine.

Lewton rounded out the cast with a capable supporting lineup, including Edith Atwater, Russell Wade, Rita Corday, Sharyn Moffett, Donna Lee, Robert Clarke, Bill Williams and Mary Gordon. Wade, who had appeared in *The Leopard Man* and co-starred with Richard Dix in *The Ghost Ship*, was the only actor Lewton considered for the Fettes role. Another child actress, Ann Carter, who had worked with Wise in *The Curse of the Cat People*, was considered, but lost out to Moffett, as Georgina. Atwater provided the necessary quality of "raw

RKO Radio publicity portrait of Rita Corday as Mrs. Marsh and Russell Wade as Fettes.

sex" for Meg Cameron (noted by Lewton in his casting notes), and Corday was awarded the Mrs. Marsh part after Gwen Crawford and Audrey Long were ruled out.[17]

The budget allocated to *The Body Snatcher* totalled $194,608, with $30,000 going to Karloff on a five-week guarantee. Lewton commanded

RKO Radio publicity portrait of Bela Lugosi, wearing an alternate wardrobe, as Joseph.

$7,100, while Jack Gross claimed $2,500 for his executive duties. Wise was paid a flat $5,700 for a shooting schedule to run 18 days, including three on location at the RKO ranch in the San Fernando Valley.

As Wise prepared for the shoot, set to begin on October 25, Lewton, with less than two days remaining, was still working on a rewrite. Daniell accepted a freelance contract (for $1,500 weekly on a two-week guarantee) on the 24th, when the cast was ordered to report for the shooting of still photographs, including publicity portraits by master photographer Ernest Bachrach, who worked at RKO for three decades (from the studio's 1929 inception until its dissolution in 1959).

To shoot the film, Lewton relied on Robert De Grasse, a veteran cinematographer whose career stretched back to 1921, including such RKO classics as *Alice Adams* (1935), *Quality Street* (1937), *Vivacious Lady* (1938) and *Vigil in the Night* (1940), directed by George Stevens. After capturing Ginger Rogers with his signature compositions and lighting in *Vivacious Lady*, he repeated the process for seven more of the actress' starring vehicles, including two of her musical pairings with Fred Astaire, *Carefree* (1938) and *The Story of Vernon and Irene Castle* (1939). He lent his atmospheric style to *A Date with the Falcon* (1942), the second entry in RKO's popular low-budget detective series, and first worked with Lewton on *The Leopard Man*. During pre-production, Lewton conveyed his stylistic preference by showing De Grasse several paintings by one of his favorite British artists, William Hogarth (1697-1764), upon whose work he would draw more directly for a subsequent Karloff collaboration.

On the morning of October 25, with the cameras ready to roll, Lugosi signed his contract. Although he was scheduled for only one week, the actor was paid $3,000, much more than he received for his work in many contemporary "penny dreadfuls" at Monogram, who had released his most recent studio vehicle, *Return of the Ape Man* (1944), on July 17. (His latest role, the ignominious butler "Merkil," in the Pine-Thomas comedy potboiler *One Body Too Many* [1944], would skulk, via Paramount, onto the nation's screens on November 24.)

Wise opened *The Body Snatcher* shoot at 9 a.m. on RKO's Stage 4, in a set featuring Gray's lodgings, including a horse stable and living quarters. At 9:15, he began working with Wade and Karloff, who performed his fight scene with Daniell later in the day.

Lugosi reported to the stage the following day, but his initial appearance was not to shoot scenes, but familiarize himself with the role and fellow cast members. He returned at 9 a.m. on October 27 to act in his first setups, in which Joseph is killed by Gray (his penultimate scene in the film, and his last while the character is still living). He and Karloff were the only actors who worked on the film that day. Patiently

Boris Karloff as Gray.

working with Lugosi, Wise later admitted embarrassment over having to ask the struggling veteran for a succession of retakes. The director remembered,

> Lugosi...was not well...It was a small part. It didn't require too much out of him, but I had to kind of nurse him through the whole role, such as it was. And I always appreciated Karloff's sensitivity when it came to the scene where they played together...where the Lugosi character came to see the Karloff character. Boris was very, very gentle with him. And I always respected Karloff for that, for the sensitivity in that situation. I have heard that he [Lugosi] was on drugs at the time. I think it might have been drugs, because he was in pain, but he got through it—it was all right. But Karloff was very, very helpful in getting him through the sequence that I had to do with them.[18]

Neither Karloff nor Lugosi was doubled while shooting the suffocation sequence. (For the more violent, fatal altercation involving Gray and MacFarlane, stuntmen Paul Stader and John Daheim substituted for Karloff and Daniell, although studio records do not indicate who doubled whom.) At 5:55 p.m., Wise sent Karloff home and then worked with Lugosi for another 45 minutes, likely to shoot several close-ups.

In *Bela Lugosi and Boris Karloff*, Gregory Mank explains,

> Tellingly, Bela Lugosi never visited RKO's Edinburgh set in the Valley. By the time *The Body Snatcher* company reported there, he'd already completed his small role. Nor would he share in the praise and glory that greeted...the greatest box office hit of the Lewton horrors, supercharging Boris Karloff's standing as one of Hollywood's top character stars.
>
> Yet Bela's mere presence in this powerful, moving, classic film—more so than its artistry, poetry and brilliance—gives *The Body Snatcher* its major distinction in

Bela Lugosi as Joseph, in a scene cut from the film.

Hollywood history. For this was the final union of Boris Karloff and Bela Lugosi, and the dynamic at play was both unforgettably fine and profoundly sad.[19]

In his brief role, Lugosi gives a convincing, moving and noteworthy performance. "He was a little vague," Wise added. "He was not quite on it—which was all right for the role, because he played a not very bright guy… I think his whole mental and emotional condition maybe helped to contribute to that."[20]

On the morning of Saturday, October 28, Wise shot the confrontation scene between MacFarlane and Gray on the Hobbs Public House set, where Lugosi, who had the day off, made an unexpected appearance. Oddly, the actor called a press conference to announce that he and his estranged wife, Lillian, were planning a reconciliation. Gregory Mank notes,

If this were true, one wonders why... Bela wasn't home in North Hollywood enjoying his reunion... Perhaps he was so abashed by his poor showing the previous day that—unable to compete with Karloff professionally in this arena—he once again, as with [Universal's] *Black Friday* [1940], arranged a little sideshow, this time a domestic saga.... Lillian... didn't actually move for a dismissal of the divorce suit until March 8, 1945. One might have expected that, if the happy news had been genuine, Bela would have shown a new energy and spirit as he continued on *The Body Snatcher*. Come his return to the set, however, and he was back in the doldrums. Russell Wade began working with Bela the week of October 30 and remembered Lugosi as "kind of in another world," "not with it," "seeming very old" and "pretty far gone."[21]

Russell Wade as Fettes and Bela Lugosi as Joseph, in a scene cut from the film.

Mank also describes a scene involving Lugosi that was shot on October 31, but cut from the film prior to release:

> [From the script] "Joseph at the desk. He has the account book open before him and with index finger moving from letter to letter, he is laboriously but silently spelling out the words. Suddenly he hears footsteps behind him on the stairs and quickly slams the book and begins dusting the desk." The scene called for Fettes to ask Joseph where Gray the cabman lived, and Joseph to insinuate a bribe. "I'd gladly run with a message, sir, for a florin," Lugosi was to say. "It's not much, considering it's Sunday." Fettes finds Joseph distasteful and goes himself. This scene ended up on the cutting room floor. A production still survives.[22]

Lugosi remained quiet during his brief participation in the production, mustering all his energy to develop a convincing and moving characterization. He spent most of his off-camera time alone, often resting in his dressing room until assistant director Harry Scott called him back to the set.

The stunning, terrifying scene that concludes the film, constructed carefully from Stevenson's own descriptive prose, was shot by two directors. On October 27 and 28, the exteriors were directed by Mark Robson with a second unit (including cinematographer Harold Stein, who shot the footage day-for-night) at the Corrigan Ranch. Wade (who, suffering from a high fever, worked on only one of the days) was joined in the scene by stuntmen Archie Butler and Allan Lee (doubling for Karloff and Daniell, respectively). Wise filmed the shots of MacFarlane and Gray inside the coach, with technicians soaking Daniell and a stripped-down, shrouded Karloff with studio rain, on November 13 (Stevenson's birthday) and 15.

The most unpleasant experience of Lugosi's five-day stretch occurred as he finished up on Thursday, November 2. The performance involved a dip into a "brine vat," the destination of Joseph after he is "burked" by Gray. At 4 p.m., unable to use a double, he waited as the water was heated prior to his descent. De Grasse then framed him in medium close-up as his submerged head was lifted from the water by

Publicity shot of Boris Karloff as Gray, shouldering a "subject."

Daniell and observed by Wade. Wise elaborated, "Lugosi did have to immerse himself into the brine vat, and he did it willingly as any good professional would do. We had no problem. I think I had to make it only once or twice—but it is Lugosi who did that particular bit in the picture."[23] By 6:30 p.m., Bela had completed his arduous final scene, as one of Dr. MacFarlane's salted subjects.

Although in constant pain, Karloff refused to let it show, thoroughly enjoying his excellent role and the company of a talented and friendly cast and crew. On one occasion, he had more fun than usual, as described by Gregory Mank:

> RKO treated a squad of soldiers to a studio tour, and ushered them onto the set of *The Body Snatcher*. The men were thrilled at the prospect of seeing the great Boris Karl-

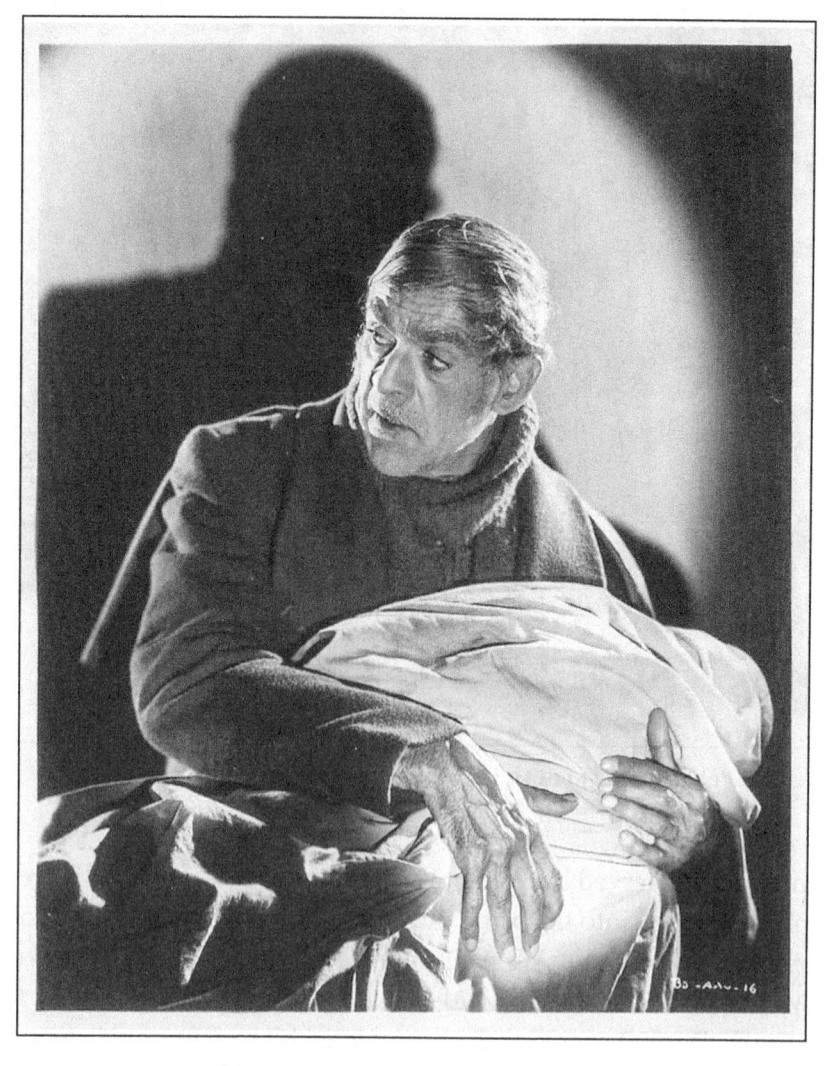

Publicity portrait of Boris Karloff as Gray.

off, and as Wise called "action," Karloff made his entrance, in top hat and with a "body" over his shoulder, smiling wickedly at the camera. As soon as Wise called, "Cut!" Boris merrily plopped down the dummy, looked at the awestruck troops, and grinned [paraphrasing one of his lines in the script]: "Goddammit, this thing is heavy!"

The soldiers roared with laughter at the surprise profanity.[24]

The first of two location excursions to the RKO ranch occurred on November 8, when Wise filmed scenes utilizing three sets, designated "Greyfriar's Churchyard," "the Edinburgh Street" and the "Street by Gray's." For the sequence that opens the film, Karloff, Wade, Mary Gordon, the uncredited bit actor who plays the marching drummer, and 27 extras reported at 9 a.m. Daniell and 14-year-old musical prodigy Donna Lee [O'Leary] joined the cast later in the day, and they worked with Wade until late evening.

Filming resumed at the studio late the following morning, with Daniell, Atwater, Corday and Moffett. Karloff joined them at 6 p.m. and, 30 minutes later, he and Wade were at the ranch with Wise, to shoot setups in the alley outside Gray's lodgings, including the stark, atmospherically staged murder of the street singer, as described in Lewton's screenplay:

> It is a long, deserted street. At the near end a lantern on a house wall casts a sphere of dim radiance… From behind the camera comes the Street Singer, walking slowly, singing and rattling her begging bowl. She walks on. Just before her figure is lost in the darkness, from behind the camera can be heard the clop-clop of hoofs, the creak of carriage springs, and the rolling wheels of Gray's cab. As the singer disappears completely into the darkness, the cab goes past the camera. It, too, disappears into the darkness. The CAMERA HOLDS. The sound of the carriage ceases. A moment later, the song of the Street Singer comes to an abrupt, choked end.

Although the entire scene was captured in a single, unedited long shot, Karloff played it himself, piloting the hansom cab down the street and into the misty shadows of the Edinburgh night. At 11:30 p.m., he was back at RKO, from which he then departed for the more familiar darkness surrounding his estate in Coldwater Canyon.

Publicity portrait of Boris Karloff as Gray, brandishing his implement of death and "resurrection."

Three days over schedule (and slightly over-budget at $217,448.86), Wise completed the shooting on Friday, November 17, 1944. Although the Greyfriars set, incorporating a portion of the cathedral built for *The Hunchback of Notre Dame* (1939), was located at the RKO ranch, Karloff performed his final scene on a facsimile constructed in the studio.

Filmed by De Grasse in heavy shadows with a mobile camera, the killing of "Robbie," the little Cairn Terrier (canine actor "Rex"), was

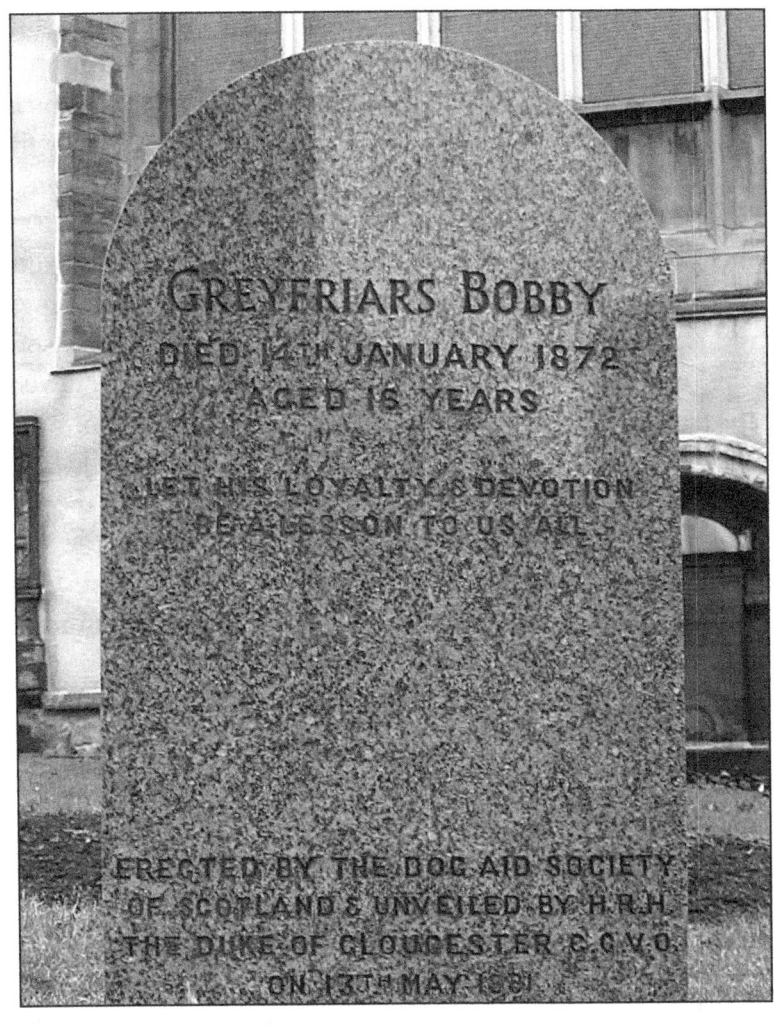

Greyfriars Bobby headstone, Greyfriars Kirkyard, Edinburgh.

the final dastardly act of Cabman Gray carried out by the actor, who left RKO at 10 p.m. that night. Lewton based "Robbie" on "Greyfriars Bobby," a Skye Terrier and contemporary (1855-1872) of Stevenson, who guarded the grave of his departed owner for a total of 14 years, faithfully remaining at Greyfriars Kirkyard until his own death. A popular version of the story identifies an Edinburgh City Police night watchman named *John Gray* as the dog's owner. When Gray died, Bobby took up permanent residence in the kirkyard, becoming widely known throughout the Old Town. (Naturally, alternate versions have been offered in attempts to debunk this sentimental favorite.)

Henry T. Hutton's nonfiction account of the events was published in Edinburgh in 1902, followed by Indiana-born writer-teacher Eleanor Stackhouse Atkinson's novel *Greyfriars Bobby* in 1912. (The latter, which altered the story considerably, was adapted for a Disney film in 1961). In a bit of dramatic sadism, Lewton turned the situation on its head, depicting the loyal grave watcher being bludgeoned to death by Karloff's John Gray before he disinters the deceased son of the mourning Mrs. McBride. (There stands in Edinburgh a pub called Greyfriars Bobby, located across from the kirkyard, where tour guides spend a great deal of time describing a schmaltzy version of the tale to visitors. Perhaps Lewton had heard this story one time too many.)

Though the historical Bobby was a Skye, named after the Isle (and later identified as an endangered dog breed), "Robbie" is a more common Cairn, one of the oldest terrier breeds, originating in the Scottish Highlands, where it became one of Caledonia's most reliable working dogs. Considered "ratters," the breed is exceptional at hunting down and killing all manner of rodents.

Cairns also have comprised a high percentage of canine actors throughout film and television history, including "Terry" ("Rags" in *Bright Eyes* [1934], "Rainbow" in *Fury* [1936] and "Toto" in *The Wizard of Oz* [1939], after which his name was changed to same), "Rommie" ("Moto" in *Air Force* (1943), "Piggy" in *Practically Yours* [1944] and "Flora" in *Heartbeat* [1946]), and "Danny" ("Fred" in *I Love Lucy* [1951-1957], "Snuffy" in *Pal Joey* [1957], "Muff" in *Anatomy of a Murder* [1959] and "Fremont" in *Dennis the Menace* [1959-1963]).

Prior to *The Body Snatcher*, "Rex" had appeared as "Duke" in *Penrod and His Twin Brother* and *Penrod's Double Trouble* (both 1938) at

The Body Snatcher: The Val Lewton Production • 79

One of RKO Radio's most memorable publicity portraits
of Boris Karloff as Gray.

Warner Bros., where he also played himself in the short "Famous Movie Dogs" (1940), and as "Rajah" in RKO's *Two Thoroughbreds* (1939). His fatal graveyard encounter with Karloff has enshrined his memory in horror-film history.

At the studio wrap party, Karloff, provided with a stack of photographs by the publicity department, graciously inscribed them as mementos for his co-workers. Having thought of him as a "type" prior to directing *The Body Snatcher*, Wise, who dined at his Coldwater Canyon home on one occasion, had quite a different impression when the shoot ended:

> I realized how much more there was to him than those monster creatures with which he had been identified so strongly. I think [he] was absolutely first-rate... an excellent actor... And then to go to his home, to see his lovely home with books all over the place. And to talk to him, such a fine, fine, knowledge, fine background. Well read, well educated. It was such a contrast—his whole being and his own personal life to what you were accustomed to seeing on the screen.[25]

Of his experience working with Henry Daniell, Karloff later said, "[He] was a pro, a real honest-to-goodness pro. There was no rubbish with him, no faking." Wise admitted, "Daniell was marvellous to work with. One of my best experiences with a top character actor—he was just brilliant." Russell Wade claimed, "It was very hard for me to keep up with Henry Daniell, a very fine actor, and on the cold side as a person," and Rita Corday concurred that he "was a marvellous actor—a very intense man, even off-screen."[26]

Assigned to the film by RKO musical director Constantin Bakaleinikoff, composer Roy Webb incorporated several traditional Scottish songs into his evocative score (an element that would have appealed to Stevenson). The Street Singer, called a "wild lassie from the Highlands" by Fettes, performs the "Jacobite tribute" song "Will Ye No Come Back Again?" ["Bonnie Charlie"] (early 1800s) by Carolina Oliphant (Lady Nairne), "When Ye Gang Awa', Jamie" ["The Duke of Athol"] (published in 1827) by William Vincent Wallace, and "We'd Better Bide a Wee" (the most familiar version of which postdates 1831). Sir Walter Scott's "The Bonnets of Bonnie Dundee" (1825) is sung by a quartet of revellers at the Fishers Tryst. Other musical characters include Fettes, who whistles his way toward Greyfriars Kirkyard, a young lad singing as he roasts the pig in the Hobbs Public House fireplace, and Gray, who vocalizes, in darkly humorous fashion, to Joseph about the murderous activities of Burke and Hare.

In an interview with *The Morning Telegraph*, Lewton wisely admitted that his frugal reuse of sets from *The Hunchback of Notre Dame* was enhanced atmospherically by his inclusion of these Scottish songs. Greatly attentive to this element, he personally supervised Donna Lee's recording sessions and later accompanied her to the makeup department, where he insisted "she receive an 1831 mouth, rather than a 'lipsticky' 1944 one."[27]

On December 1, just two weeks after Wise wrapped *The Body Snatcher*, which now was in the cutting room, Karloff returned to RKO, to shoot *Isle of the Dead* with Lewton and director Mark Robson, who completed production in 11 days. On February 21, 1945, Karloff, in Honolulu starring as Jonathan Brewster in a "road" version of *Arsenic and Old Lace* with the U.S. Army entertainment section in the Central Pacific, wrote to the studio, asking for two 16mm prints of *The Body Snatcher*, which had been previewed for the press a week earlier. Having contributed a live stage performance to entertain the troops, he also wanted to show them one of his cinematic efforts.

4
Exploiting *The Body Snatcher*

ON FEBRUARY 10, 1945, Terry Turner, head of RKO's exploitation staff, had arrived in the Midwest to initiate advance campaigns for two features. After meeting with Dick Powell in Chicago, to discuss the actor-director's personal appearance tour for the *film noir* thriller *Murder My Sweet* (1945), Turner headed to St. Louis, where *The Body Snatcher* was scheduled to open its "world premiere run" at Fanchon and Marco's Missouri Theatre on Valentine's Day. Established in 1920 at 626 N. Grand Boulevard, the Missouri was one of the nation's largest movie houses, comfortably seating 3,558 patrons. Following the Lewton premiere, Turner returned to the Windy City, joining Powell for a February 22 engagement at the RKO Palace.

The publicity campaign, headlining "Robert Louis Stevenson's Nerve-Tingling Tale of Terror" and "The Screen's Sensational Scarer... Karloff, the Body Snatcher, a Maniacal Murderer Who Filled Graves and Robbed Them," advised exhibitors to perform the following ballyhoo:

> Rent an open sound truck and have a black-shrouded figure wearing a grimacing mask driven around town, with warning: "Get off the Streets! Beware! The Body Snatcher is Here!" For lobby, lay out an artificial grassy mound re-

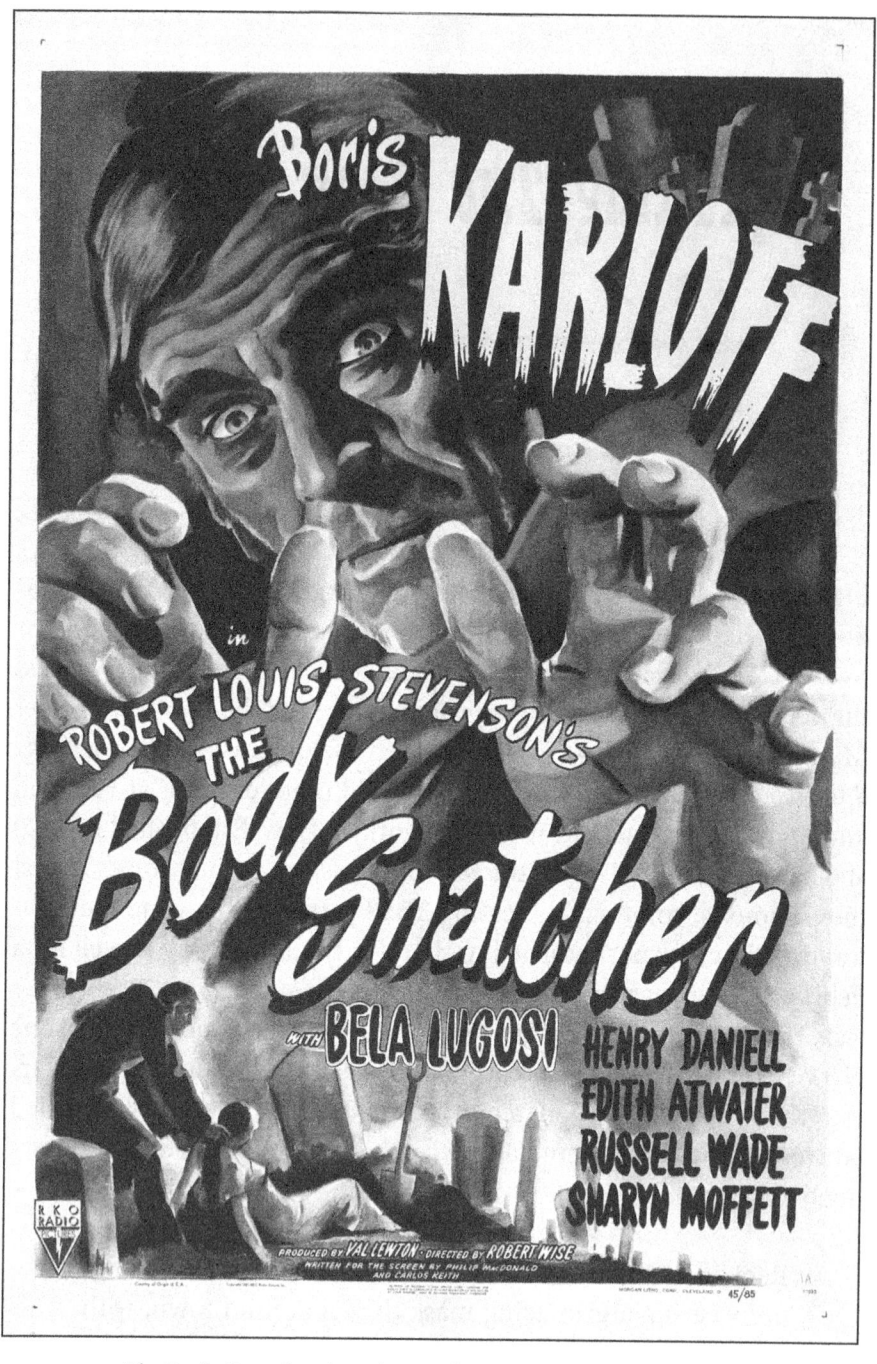

The Body Snatcher (1945) one-sheet poster, with artwork of Boris Karloff by William Rose.

sembling a grave with headstone, alongside of it stand a life-size cut of Karloff with caption: CAN YOUR NERVES TAKE IT? Then have arrow pointing to a first-aid depot near entrance, with white garbed employee in attendance. Print throwaways: "We Dare You to Spend a Night at the_____as the Body Snatcher's Guest."[1]

On the day of the Missouri Theatre premiere, the 398th Bombardment Group of the U.S. Army Air Forces carried out a B-17 carpet-bombing, dropping about 152 tons of explosives on Prague, capital of the Nazi-occupied Protectorate of Bohemia and Moravia, destroying approximately 100 houses and historical sites, and damaging 200 others. Casualties numbered 701, with 1,184 wounded. The "blind attack," carried out using radar after the group took off from its base at RAF Nuthampstead, in Hertfordshire, England, was later identified as the result of equipment malfunction and high winds producing a "dead reckoning navigational error of some 70 miles." Obscured by clouds, Prague, which, from the air, closely resembled the intended target, Dresden, a German industrial center and defensive area, tragically was hit by mistake. (Later, the pilots expressed their regret over the accident, and the United States was billed for extensive damage to the historical buildings. The air raid was utilized for propaganda purposes by both Germany and the subsequent communist regime of Czechoslovakia.)

Back in St. Louis, Terry Turner's "new idea" of "plattering" *The Body Snatcher* event was carried out. Arranging for "the placing of a radio recording machine on the stage apron," the exploitation chief captured the soundtrack and responses of the patrons, who were "not aware that the records were being made." Six platters, made by a local company, were required to capture all 78 minutes of *The Body Snatcher*. *Showmen's Trade Review* explained,

> Turner figured that the actual recording of an audience's reaction would be of inestimable value to producers, writers, directors and artists, as well as the sales staffs of the film companies, since they could learn more about what they are selling, what points to publicize, what errors to avoid in the future…

Turner indicated that this procedure for obtaining audience reaction will be limited to action pictures and not to dramas and heavier efforts. He added that the chief value of the new plan is that it gauges the views of those who have the last and most important say about the success of a picture, the men and women who pay to see it.

Sets of the completed recordings were shipped to the Hollywood and New York offices of RKO, "for careful study by important studio and sales executives." If approved, Turner planned to distribute additional copies to all RKO domestic exchanges.[2]

Motion Picture Herald published a detailed account of the world-premiere festivities:

> Backed up by a "scream contest," street and lobby ballyhoo, and extensive newspaper and radio advertising, the campaign put on to herald the opening of "The Body Snatcher" at the Missouri Theatre in St. Louis is one that will be long remembered by the citizens of that city.
>
> Manager Harry Crawford of the Missouri will also have cause to remember by virtue of a warrant served to him for disturbing the peace. An elaborate set piece placed atop the marquee emitted a howl of a lonesome dog at one-second intervals. It was the noise from this ballyhoo [to] which tenants objected… which drew the complaint.
>
> The theatre front and marquee were decorated appropriately during the current engagement of the film. A mechanical set piece, 15 ft. square, showed Karloff removing the body of a woman from a grave and was installed in the lobby well in advance of the playdate. Skulls, mummified bats and bodies also contributed to the eerie background.
>
> An effective street ballyhoo was employed utilizing a hundred-year-old hearse filled with dummy bodies which was hauled about the city streets by two decrepit horses.
>
> The picture opened on Valentine's Day and 25,000 novel valentine heralds were distributed illustrating a bleeding heart with Karloff strangling Lugosi and the for-

mer holding a valentine with caption, "Please give me a piece of your heart."

Black and white dash cards were posted on all city buses and trolley cars against a background of skull and crossbones.

Radio advertising included spot announcements and transcriptions and a novel "scream contest" sponsored by station WMTV. Entrants were obtained and the contestants after hearing a special Karloff recording were given the go ahead signal to scream. The winner was adjudged in the control room as the one whose screams reached the highest pitch and was given a booking on a spook show which shared program honors with the picture.[3]

All the elaborate goings-on at the Missouri helped rake in a total of $15,000 (filling the 3,558 seats at 50 to 60 cents each) during the film's

The Body Snatcher (1945) style "A" half sheet poster.

opening week, receiving *Variety*'s declaration of "good biz" at the box office.[4] For the second week, receipts, according to the trade publication, were "trim[med to] $9,000 after big $15,000 first stanza."[5] Two weeks later, the haul had taken another precipitous dive, to $5,000.[6]

On February 16, *Motion Picture Daily*'s Thalia Bell reported,

> Addicts of the gruesome will find [the] production to their taste. ...[I]t has Boris Karloff as a graverobber in Scotland in 1831. Bela Lugosi contributes a macabre bit, and Henry Daniell... turns in a matchless performance, sensitively shaded and completely convincing. Robert Wise's direction creates an unbroken mood of somberness and suspense, and the music, by Roy Webb... makes good use of Scotch folk songs to enhance the picture's eeriness.... Altogether, "The Body Snatcher" is far superior to the general run of horror films.[7]

The following day, *Showmen's Trade Review* enthusiastically pitched the production to exhibitors:

> Here is a real exploitation natural for mystery-action-horror fans. Karloff, Lugosi for the marquee, Robert Louis Stevenson story for school-library plugs, "see it from the beginning" and "we dare you" copy for ads...
>
> This is one of the best-made horror-dramas in the many years of the Karloff-Lugosi teamwork. The story is credible, coherently told, and contains some excellent characterizations. The cast is well chosen and the direction is superb. The picture is too gruesome for children, however. One of its interesting features is the method of giving a class treatment to a rip-roaring spine chiller. The photography is well molded to the mood required and there are several sequences which will bring the most blasé horror fan right out on the edge of the seat....Karloff has a remarkable role and delivers one of his finest acting jobs to date. The picture offers a great opportunity for exploitation and the horror angle can be capitalized to the

fullest. The film is perfect for action houses and deserves a 50/50 billing in most double-bill situations.[8]

Another influential trade publication, *The Film Daily*, concurred, singling out Daniell for praise:

> Vastly different from the usual far-fetched themes starring the Karloff-Lugosi combination, "The Body Snatcher," film version of an excellent short story by Robert Louis Stevenson, comes as a special treat for those who seek entertainment of the hair-raising variety. With all due recognition to Karloff's fine characterization, Henry Daniell's impressive performance is outstanding. Aimed at better-than-average audience appeal, a better-than-average budget for this type of film is evident; and the direction is noteworthy for its lip-biting suspense…
> DIRECTION, Fine. PHOTOGRAPHY, Excellent.[9]

On February 24, *Box Office* also recommended the unusually inventive *The Body Snatcher* to exhibitors:

> Its title and the marquee appeal of two recognized, past master chill dispensers should attract the horror play fans in large and profitable droves. But they are going to be surprised, if nothing more, at what they see on the screen. It is an intelligently produced, rather artistic screen version of the Robert Louis Stevenson book [sic] about early 19th century medicos and their criminal activities in obtaining cadavers for dissecting and research.[10]

That same day, *Box Office* also reported,

> Why is Perry (The Mallet) Lieber superstitious? On the same day he previewed "The Body Snatcher" for the press he appeared before the War Labor Board in the Screen Publicists Guild contract hearing.
> It was the 13th of the month.[11]

(Illinois-native Lieber left a Chicago advertising agency job to join RKO in 1930. Three years after being so affected by *The Body Snatcher*, he began a long-term association with another acquisitionist of sorts, Howard Hughes, when the billionaire oil man-aviator-film producer purchased the studio in 1948.)

Echoing the *Box Office* assessment of the film, *Harrison's Reports* enthused,

> Skilfully produced and directed…it is far superior to pictures of this type.…Boris Karloff, as the blackmailing graverobber, gives one of the best performances of his career, while Henry Daniell is not far behind him as head of the medical school; their ghoulish, maniacal doings keep one on the edge of his seat. Unlike most horror pictures,

The Body Snatcher (1945) lobby card: Sharyn Moffett as Georgina and Boris Karloff as Gray.

this one does not resort to the fantastic for its chills and shudders; it makes sense…

Too horrifying for children.[12]

On March 10, *Box Office* reported that Wally Heim, a United Artists' exploitation man in St. Louis, ignited "railroad torpedo flares atop the marquee of the Missouri Theatre to get around the [wartime] brownout regulations when 'The Body Snatcher' first opened." Heim, whose action was approved by the local director of public safety, had offered to pay the salary of a city fire fighter to observe the flaming flares, but was advised that the vigilance of the theatre maintenance man would suffice. The report continued, "With Grand Blvd. almost completely darkened because of the brownout the burning flares grabbed a lot of attention. Flares last for about ten minutes each and are easily replaced. The flares do not violate the brownout regulations, local officials ruled."[13]

In late March, RKO chose five new films to be trade shown nationally in the company's 32 exchange centers from April 16-19: *Those Endearing Young Charms*, *China Sky*, *The Body Snatcher*, *Tarzan and the Amazons* and *Zombies on Broadway*. Featuring Bela Lugosi as Professor Paul Renault, *Zombies*, co-starring the comedy duo of Wally Brown and Alan Carney, went into general release two weeks before *The Body Snatcher*.

On May 8, 1945, World War II ended in Europe with the total and unconditional surrender of Germany. At RKO eight days later, with *The Body Snatcher* beginning to menace screens nationwide, Russell Wade answered a letter from an admirer, who had requested a signed photograph. On official studio letterhead, he wrote,

> May I thank you for your letter which was greatly appreciated. I am hoping you will see and enjoy my next pictures, "The Body Snatcher" and "The Most Dangerous Game" when they come to your theatre.….It gives me great pleasure to consider you a fan and I shall hope to deserve your continued loyalty. Very truly yours, Russell Wade.[14]

Russell Wade handwritten letter to a fan, in which he mentions *The Body Snatcher*, May 16, 1945.

(Directed by Robert Wise, *A Game of Death*, a remake of RKO's *The Most Dangerous Game* [1932], based on the story by Richard Connell, was released on November 23, 1945 [Karloff's birthday, incidentally], six months after *The Body Snatcher* went into general distribution.)

On the same day that Wade mailed his letter, reception of *The Body Snatcher* hit a censorial roadblock when the National Legion of Decency slapped the film with its undesirable "B" classification: "Morally Objectionable in Part for All" (just one step up from the dreaded "C": Condemned) due to "excessive gruesomeness." By contrast, the organization considered PRC's *The Missing Corpse* and Universal's *Swing Out, Sister* "A-II": "Morally Unobjectionable for Adults and Adolescents," and Columbia's *Boston Blackie Booked on Suspicion* and Republic's *The Magnificent Rogue* "A-I": "Morally Unobjectionable for General Patronage."

Prior to the Legion's classification, *The Body Snatcher* had been "rejected" outright by Sergeant L. S. White, acting director of the Chicago police censor board. (He, like Stevenson originally, must have found the story "too horrid" for public consumption.) During April, the board had inspected 82 films, condemning Lewton's Stevenson adaptation, ordering *Zombies on Broadway* "pinked," and specifying cuts for 15 others.[15] For the board's May program, Sergeant White was replaced by Lieutenant Timothy Lyne, who accepted 82 new titles, but classified seven "for adults," primarily horror films, in addition to Columbia's *Kiss and Tell*. Reconsidering *The Body Snatcher*, Lyne issued an "adult permit," but maintained the board's rejection of *Crime, Inc.* and *Dillinger*.[16]

When *The Body Snatcher* played on a double bill with *The Brighton Strangler* at Chicago's Grand Theatre on W. North Avenue, RKO's representative invited city coroner Cal Brodie to attend a screening, an offer he kindly accepted.[17] *Variety* was impressed with the venue's first-week performance, which grossed a "snappy" $10,000 (filling 1,150 seats at 55 to 95 cents each). The two thrillers earned another $8,000 the following week.[18]

On May 25, *The Body Snatcher* opened at the Rialto Theatre on Broadway. John McManus wrote in *New York PM Reviews*,

> *The Body Snatcher* inherits class from its Robert Louis Stevenson parentage; it has the distinction, like many an ancient and honorable British ballad, of being a shocker with an edifying background of fact; and it has the advantage of production by Val Lewton, the *Cat People* originator... Bo-

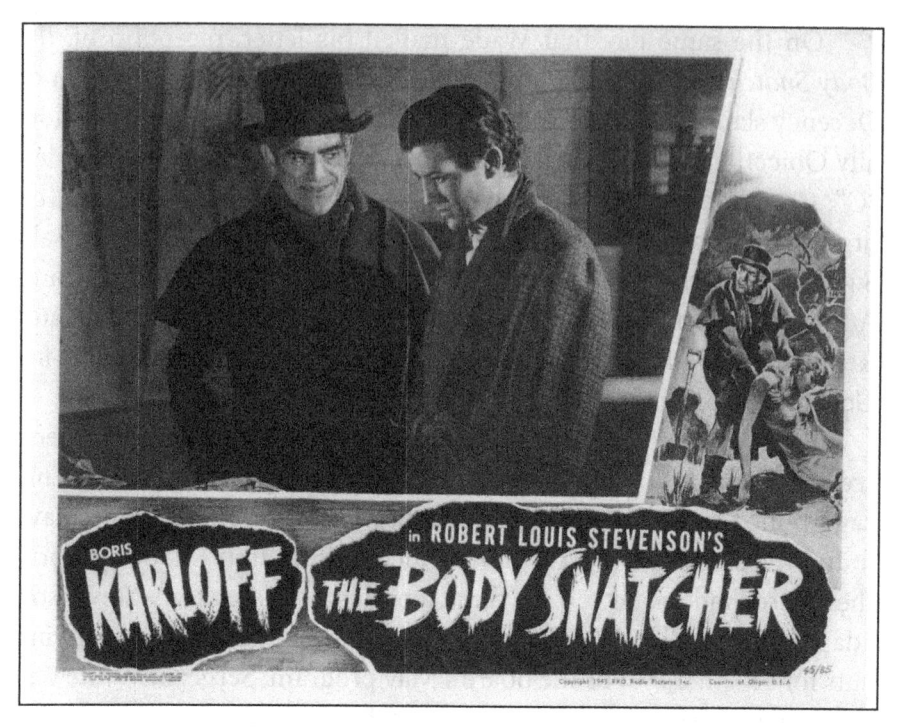

The Body Snatcher (1945) lobby card: Boris Karloff as Gray and Russell Wade as Fettes.

ris Karloff… makes an evildoer's holiday of his part… *The Body Snatcher*, if you are one for well-told legends, for balladry or just for shockers by preference, is something you won't want to miss.[19]

The popular movie magazine *Photoplay*, in its signature style, also recommended *The Body Snatcher*:

> Brother, check your hair at the door lest it rise right off your head and go sailing way, for here's a horror number would scare a totem pole into splinters.
>
> Boris Karloff, who snatches dead bodies (if some aren't dead Boris sees to it they get that way) for the medical school of Henry Daniell, seems to us more horribly wonderful than ever.

Russell Wade turns in a swell performance as the harassed young medical student who eventually gets embroiled in the unholy mess. And, oh yes, Bela Lugosi creeps in and out for a quick boo or two. But it's Karloff and Daniell who really make the picture for our money.

Your Reviewer Says: This is a swell scare 'em show.[20]

The May issue of *New Movies: The National Board of Review Magazine* highly praised the film: "Robert Louis Stevenson's story of grave robbers comes alive in all its macabre eeriness in this smart, adroit film.... The payoff is brilliantly hair-raising. Wrought with skill in direction, photography and writing, the picture transcends the run-of-the-mill 'horror film.' Henry Daniell and Boris Karloff give unusually good performances."[21] The following month, the publication ran a full, perceptive review by "A.B.":

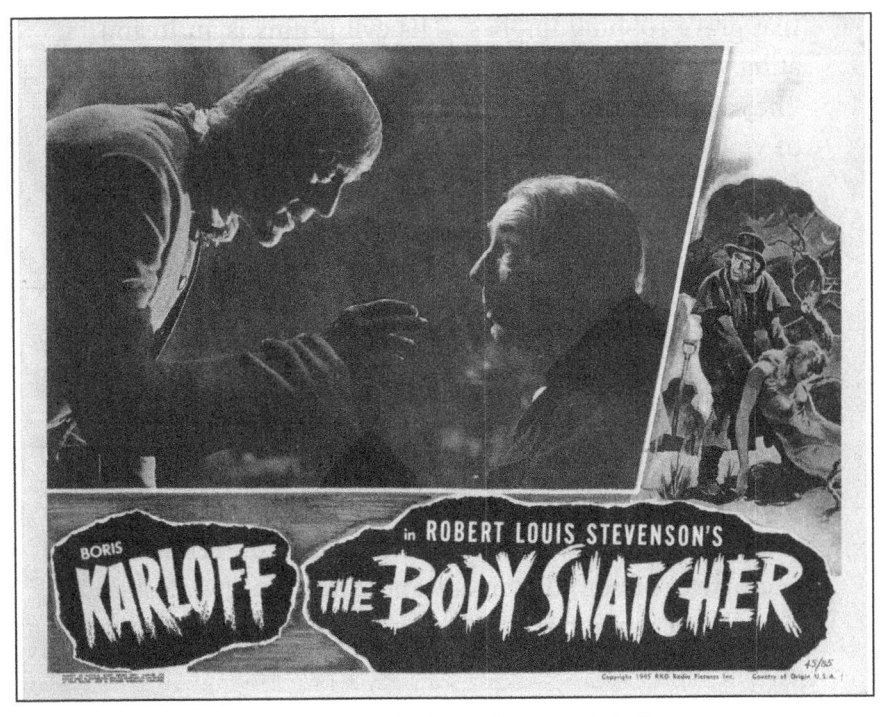

The Body Snatcher (1945) lobby card: Boris Karloff as Gray and Bela Lugosi as Joseph.

It is not often that a "horror film" transcends its class but *The Body Snatcher* does it hands down. Its serious theme and historical background give it a dignity that is not found in movies conceived to scare you out of your seat. And the skill with which the movie is made places it in the list of those none too frequent products that may be viewed as examples of cinematic art. Val Lewton has been making quite a name for himself ever since he produced *Cat People* in 1942. Characteristic of his films are themes that deal with the psychic aberrations of the human mind, that are mounted with imaginative settings and recorded with a knowing camera, that are intensified with a compelling usage of music and sound. *The Body Snatcher* is the study of the effect on the mind of an intelligent man of years of an almost sadistic mental persecution. The harassed doctor is not without sympathetic appeal to the audience in spite of the normal person's revulsion from all that grave robbing implies. His evil genius is an insinuatingly cruel creature with a gentle affection for animals. The cabman's persistent hounding and the final instances of violence overthrow MacFarlane's mind in the chilling finale. The action carries through the byways and abodes of the Scottish city represented by sets of a gloomy solidity and an artful evocation of being trapped and doomed…

The cast includes Boris Karloff as the cabman portraying his part with a wickedness devoid of burlesque. Bela Lugosi who, freed of his Draculesque idiom, enacts a stupid and voracious Portuguese, and Henry Daniell who brings to Doctor MacFarlane a wealth of strength and even warmth. The other members are less spectacular if no less competent. And all of them with the help of technicians and artists of sound, camera and direction give Robert Louis Stevenson's tale as handsome a film production as any top writer could wish.[22]

During the film's initial week in general release, the 594-seat Rialto, selling tickets ranging from 40 to 85 cents, hauled in nearly $11,000. The

The Body Snatcher (1945) lobby card: Henry Daniell as Dr. MacFarlane and Russell Wade as Fettes.

next week remained "strong" ($9,000) but dropped to "fair" ($6,000) for the third and final seven-day stretch.[23] At the RKO Orpheum in Kansas City, the manager, running *The Body Snatcher* and *The Brighton Strangler* double feature, continuously filled the 1,500 seats, at 45 to 65 cents each, realizing $9,000 for the week.

On June 12, the 3,200-seat Boston RKO, selling 50-cent to $1.10 tickets for *The Body Snatcher* alone (the latter price for a bill including Irene Manning and the Georgie Auld Orchestra performing on stage), estimated an impressive $26,000 for the week. *Variety*'s "Dame" reported, "A hot potpourri largely vocal and instrumental... coupled with good draw of thrill pic. packs 'em into RKO."[24] During the same week, the RKO Albee in Providence, loading 2,100 seats at 45 to 60 cents, estimated a $14,000 total.

The June issue of RKO's official "foreign sales house organ," *The Foreign Legion*, featured its publicity in seven languages: English, Hebrew,

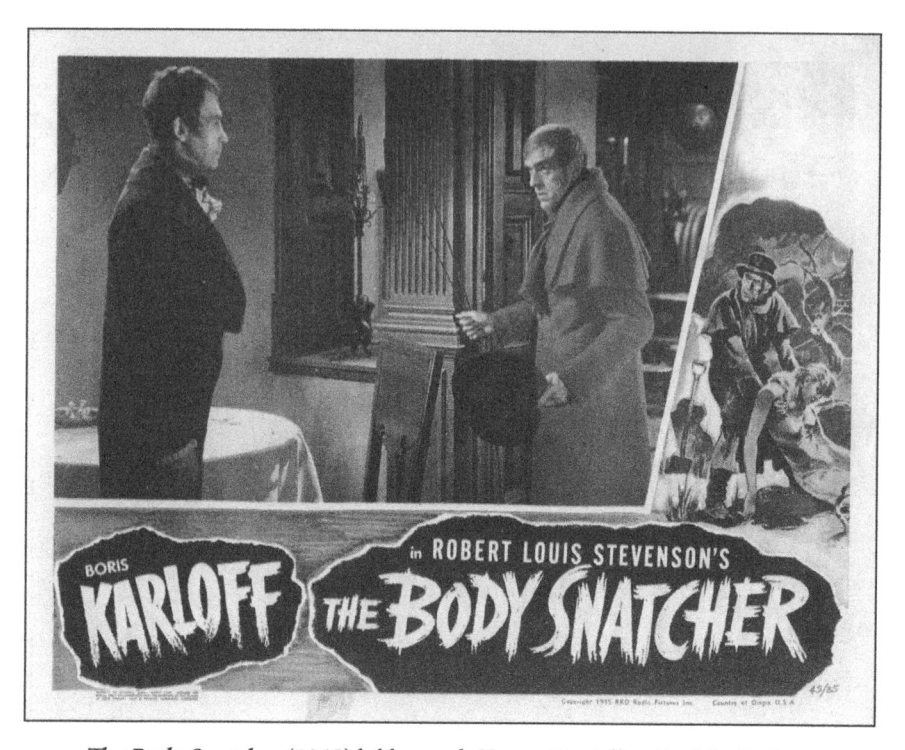

The Body Snatcher (1945) lobby card: Henry Daniell as Dr. MacFarlane and Boris Karloff as Gray.

Hindustani, Portuguese, Spanish, French and Arabic. The studio's buildup advised exhibitors to give *The Body Snatcher* "top exploitation."[25]

Meanwhile, the June 20 issue of *The Film Daily* reported, "Believe it or not, just as the United Detroit Circuit was building up its publicity campaign for RKO's 'The Body Snatcher,' an old Detroit cemetery was the scene of a grave robbery!"[26] (This bit of curious "news" likely was *part* of the "publicity campaign.")

On June 27, *Box Office* published a brief review, offering a cogent synopsis that would put a studio publicity department to shame, and providing an assessment of the film's setting that accurately describes human behavior at any time in history: "In the early 19th century, ignorance and fear confronting medical men force them to consort with graverobbers to obtain bodies for dissection. Such a man is one Edinburgh doctor, Henry Daniell. He becomes involved with a monstrous ghoul, Boris Karloff, who resorts to murder to get corpses."[27]

That week, when the film opened at the RKO Golden Gate Theatre in San Francisco, the management pitched the show as "The Big Three of Menace: Together in one horrific show." Karloff and Lugosi may have been the on-screen attraction, but on stage—in person: Peter Lorre, who joined Irene Manning and agreed to promote the picture in radio interviews. Local stations KSFO, KYA and KLX participated in the campaign, spinning records featuring Karloff speaking some choice Cabman John Gray dialogue. The theater also staged some street ballyhoo, hiring a driver to dress as Karloff and perform a buggy stunt with a "dummy body."[28]

During the first week of August, patronage for *The Body Snatcher* and *The Brighton Strangler* double feature began to taper off. Seattle's Music Hall (2,200 seats at 45 to 85 cents) grossed $5,100, and Denver's Webber (750 seats, 35 to 75 cents) fared even worse at $1,500, but faced stiff competition from the same city's Paramount (2,200 seats, 35 to 75 cents), which scored a "nice" $9,000. Philadelphia's Earle (2,760 seats at 50 to 95 cents), however, featuring Ethel Waters and the George Paxton Orchestra on stage, racked up an impressive $15,000.[29] And on August 21, Buffalo's 3000-seat 20th Century, selling 40 to 70-cent tickets, reported a respectable $9,000.[30]

Following the U.S. atomic devastation of Hiroshima and Nagasaki, the Imperial Empire of Japan had capitulated on August 15, and the official Instrument of Surrender was signed aboard the U.S.S. *Missouri* in Tokyo Bay on September 2. Two weeks later, the Louisville, Kentucky, Strand Theater (1,400 seats at 40 to 60 cents each) considered $6,500 adequate for the "good horror combo" of *The Body Snatcher* and *The Brighton Strangler*.[31]

By the time the film, on a solo bill, reached the Hamilton Theatre in Lancaster, Pennsylvania, in late September 1945, exhibition required "good old Yankee ingenuity… in the lobby display created [by] Herbert J. Thatcher," the manager, who described his elaborate efforts to a reporter for *The Exhibitor*:

> The entire display was of my creation with the exception of the painted background of trees, and I spent three weeks in between jobs completing the entire display. The figures were ordinary 18-inch dolls originally, a boy and

100 • *The Body Snatcher and the Making of a Horror Film Classic*

In this publicity still, Boris Karloff demonstrates his enthusiasm for Val Lewton's literate adaptation of Robert Louis Stevenson's macabre short story.

a girl; however, in order to get the desired effect with a girl doll, it was necessary to give her a special hair-do, close her eyes, and cut her limbs and body in such places to make it fit over the shoulders of the reproduction of Karloff.

> The figure of Karloff was still a greater problem. Originally it represented a soldier wearing a cap. Fortunately, it was made of plastic, so I was able to cut away the cap and part of the head. This had to be done in order to permit me to make a new hat out of plaster as well as a new face, long nose, sunken cheeks, pointed chin, etc., as you can see. In fact, I think I must have painted and repainted Karloff's face a half-dozen times before I got the right colors to work out best under the weird lights.[32]

Considering all the anatomical alterations that Thatcher inflicted on the figures of the girl and "Karloff," he may have drawn inspiration from the combined techniques of Dr. Knox and Dr. Frankenstein! *Motion Picture Herald* also trumpeted the manager's extensive "very realistic" efforts "depicting the star, Boris Karloff, carrying away the body of a girl, with copy reading, "See Karloff at work":

> Herb based his entire campaign on the "shock and shudder" angle of the film. A number of radio spot announcements were promoted prior to opening date and throughout the engagement. Newspaper ads were heavy with a specially drawn ad appearing the day before opening, headed by the copy reading, "O.K., Lancaster... You said you could take it... but can you?"[33]

The combined box-office receipts for *The Body Snatcher* totalled $547,000 in domestic and foreign rentals, netting a $118,000 profit for RKO Radio and giving Val Lewton the biggest financial success of his career. Some of Henry Daniell's most visible roles after *The Body Snatcher* occurred in his third Sherlock Holmes film, *Woman in Green* (1945), in which he plays the "Napoleon of Crime," Professor "Moriarity," to Rathbone's "Great Detective," and in a wide variety of television programs, including five episodes of *Thriller* (1960-1961), hosted by Boris Karloff.

Production on "Chamber of Horrors: A Tale of Bedlam," Karloff's third (and final) RKO collaboration with Lewton, began on July 18, 1945. Set at London's St. Mary's of Bethlehem Hospital in 1761, the

Atmospheric publicity portrait of Boris Karloff as Gray.

film vividly chronicles the efforts of Nell Bowen (Anna Lee), the former companion of a Tory politician, to end the sadistic reign of Apothecary General George Sims (Karloff), who charges visitors tuppence to view the "loonies" in their cages.

Playing Sims made Karloff somewhat uncomfortable, as he had to create a wantonly sadistic character capable of gaining audience sympathy. To justify Sims' iniquitous behavior, Lewton presented him as a living symbol of the deterministic views that held precedence during the Enlightenment, or "Age of Reason:" particularly the belief that a natural hierarchy placed each class of people in its "proper" place. Regardless of the personal distaste he felt for the character, Karloff gave another sterling performance for the producer, especially in his scenes with the equally talented Lee.

After *Bedlam* wrapped on August 17, 1945, Lewton intended to produce "Blackbeard," another historical picture, starring Karloff as "Captain Aguilar," an aging American pirate attempting to make a living in the area around Charleston, South Carolina. As co-written by Ardel Wray and Mark Robson, the screenplay offered him a unique character, but this version of the film was never made. Due to two deaths during 1945, those of RKO's Charles Koerner (in February) and the horror genre (following World War II), *Bedlam* became Lewton's final film for RKO and the end of his collaboration with Karloff.

In the 1949 edition of his study *The Film Till Now: A Survey of World Cinema*, acclaimed British director, film historian and critic Paul Rotha wrote,

> Val Lewton… is a producer of horror films which have achieved a vogue among intellectuals… and his *The Body Snatcher* (1945), with Boris Karloff, was almost certainly the superior of all horror films, at least in terms of literacy and mature approach. His last film, *Bedlam* (1946), also with Karloff, had a weak script, and since then he has been inactive because of illness. It is clear that Lewton's is the directing intelligence behind all films he has produced; they maintain approximately the same level of quality regardless of who writes or directs them. This quality has been achieved, moreover, on a small budget and to remarkable box-office response. Lewton's return to activity is eagerly anticipated, especially under the aegis of Dore Schary, who may be expected to permit him to handle more serious material than has fallen to his lot in the past.[34]

After signing a contract with Paramount Pictures, Lewton produced three films but felt entrapped (like one of the characters in his RKO thrillers) by the studio politics that stifled his independent creative spirit. Accepting a position with Stanley Kramer, he continued to be dogged by disappointment, the stress mounting until he suffered a heart attack. At Cedars of Lebanon Hospital in Los Angeles, wracked by anxiety, he struggled to breathe, even after being placed in an oxygen tent. The sad similarity to the fates of his cinematic characters continued to build, until he called out to the hospital staff that he was suffocating inside the enclosure.

On March 14, 1951, Val Lewton, the Russian-born writer and producer of one of world cinema's tiny handful of outstanding Robert Louis Stevenson adaptations, died from myocardial infarction. He was just 46 years old, a little more than two years and nine months older than another sensitive and ground-breaking artist at the time of his untimely demise: the Scottish author of "The Body-Snatcher."

In 1989, *Bedlam*'s Nell Bowen, Anna Lee, recalled, "As for [Boris Karloff's] relationship with Val Lewton, I know he was very fond of him. I loved Val and it was a great loss to the industry when he died so young."[35]

5
Dissecting *The Body Snatcher*

CREDITS

Director: Robert Wise; **Producer**: Val Lewton; **Executive Producer**: Jack J. Gross; **Screenplay**: Philip MacDonald, Carlos Keith [Val Lewton]; **Based on the Story** by Robert Louis Stevenson; **Director of Photography**: Robert De Grasse; **Editor**: J. R. Whittredge; **Musical Score**: Roy Webb; **Musical Director**: Constantin Bakaleinikoff; **Art Directors**: Albert S. D'Agostino, Walter E. Keller; **Set Decorators**: Darrell Silvera, John Sturtevant; **Sound Directors**: Bailey Fesler, Terry Kellum; **Camera Operator**: Charles Burke; **Assistant Camera**: Tex Wheaton; **Special Effects**: Vernon L. Walker, Lynn Dunn; **First Assistant Director**: Harry Scott; **Second Assistant Director**: Nate Levinson; **Script Clerk**: Pat Betz; **Men's Wardrobe**: Hans Bohnstedt; **Ladies' Wardrobe**: Mary Tate; **Makeup**: Frank LaRue, Mel Berns; **Costumes**: Renié; **Hairdresser**: Fay Smith; **Gaffer**: Leo Green; **Best Boy**: Frank Healy; **First Grip**: Marvin Wilson; **Second Grip**: Harry Dagliesh; **First Propman**: Milt James; **Second Propman**: Dean Morgan; **Boom**: D. Lent; **Laborers**: Joe Farquhar, Fred Kenny; **Painter**: Joe Haecker; **Dialogue Director**: Mrs. Charlot; **Production Company** and **Distributor**: RKO Radio Pictures, Inc.; **Release Date**: February 16, 1945; **Running Time**: 78 minutes.

The Body Snatcher (1945) style "B" half sheet poster.

Cast: Boris Karloff (Cabman John Gray), Bela Lugosi (Joseph), Henry Daniell (Dr. MacFarlane), Edith Atwater (Meg Cameron), Russell Wade (Donald Fettes), Rita Corday (Mrs. Marsh), Sharyn Moffett (Georgina Marsh), Donna Lee (Street Singer), Robert Clarke (Richardson, Medical Student), Carl Kent (Gilchrist, Medical Student), Bill Williams (Survis, Medical Student), Jack Welch (Boy), Larry Wheat (Salesman on Street), Mary Gordon (Mrs. Mary McBride), Jim Moran (Angus, Horse Trader), Aina Constant (Maidservant), Ted Billings (Townsman), Bobby Burns (Mourner), Milton Kibbee (Dan), Ethan Laidlaw (Pub Patron).

Robert Louis Stevenson never saw a movie. If he had lived into the 20th century, at least long enough to witness the Great War and the first film adaptations of his stories, he might have had difficulty deciding which of the two he disliked more. If he had struggled on a bit longer, he might have been quite surprised, even horrified, to see his name attached to so many cinematic works.

Now in its second century of existence, the motion picture medium has maintained a general unfaithfulness to Stevenson. Though biographer David Daiches notes that "the whole attitude displayed by Stevenson to his art is thoroughly congenial to the modern mind," the modern art of the cinema, born during the year in which Stevenson died, rarely has accommodated that attitude.[1] His distinguished, varied and often timeless works arguably have been bastardized more flagrantly than those of Edgar Allan Poe and Sir Arthur Conan Doyle. His acute perception of human behavior has been represented adequately by only a few film adaptations, namely Paramount's *Dr. Jekyll and Mr. Hyde* (1931), Agamemnon-Turner Network Television's *Treasure Island* (1990) and—happily for our purposes—*The Body Snatcher*.

In *Dreams of Darkness*, Professor J. P. Telotte's 1985 thematic study of the Val Lewton films, he writes,

> *The Body Snatcher* explores the deal we feel we might make with death, whereby we try to take its measure and turn it to life's account, all the while maintaining a firm footing in the realm of the living and its dayworld perspective. It is a pact that, the film suggests, only the rational mind with its insistence on its own controlling powers could conceive of. Instead of our common, archetypal attraction to an underworld such as James Hillman describes, "the innate urge to go below appearances to the 'invisible connection' and hidden constitution" of psychic life, then *The Body Snatcher* details a disturbing fascination with the underground, as man turns his attention to the depths of the grave in an effort to nourish physical life by, as it were, feeding upon death.
>
> As its title implies, *The Body Snatcher* presents a proscribed desire for the human body and a compulsion to violate the depths to which it is usually consigned at death.[2]

Addressing the story, Telotte adds,

> Like few films in the [Lewton] series, *The Body Snatcher* draws the outline for the exploration from a well-known literary work, Robert Louis Stevenson's tale, "The Body-

Snatcher." In bringing this Victorian horror story to the screen, Lewton assumed the task of reworking its structure and characterizations himself... What he had to work with was by no means a simplistic horror tale; "The Body-Snatcher" is a multilevel story, structurally reminiscent of Henry James's *The Turn of the Screw*. It employs an anonymous narrator to introduce an acquaintance named Fettes and to recount this character's history as it was related to him. Distanced by time from the actions he reports, this narrator inexplicably breaks off his account with one horrific scene, a grotesque vision or visitation once experienced by Fettes...

What probably attracted Lewton and his colleagues to Stevenson's tale is its preeminent concern with the human psyche, rather than with the ghouls and monsters which so permeated the horror genre. Also, it offered the possibility of a doubling motif, less starkly stated than in Stevenson's more famous horror story, *Dr. Jekyll and Mr. Hyde*, yet similar to that developed in *The Seventh Victim* and *The Ghost Ship*.[3]

Some earlier commentators on *The Body Snatcher* criticized Lewton and Wise's overemphasis on its literary and historical aspects, a viewpoint ignoring so much that is essentially "Stevensonian." Joel Siegel considered the opening "too detailed to suit its function,"[4] yet these images (like other visual and aural elements throughout the film) vividly convey the richness of the Edinburgh period so important to the context of the story and the history that inspired Stevenson to write it. Robert Wise explained, "Maybe some of the details could have been a little less thorough, might have been sloughed off a bit, but I believe that the atmosphere that's created by some of those 'unregistering' bits of detail is very pervasive and gets to the actors; it influences them, therefore it influences the whole scene."[5]

Telotte identifies the effectiveness of this visual introduction:

> "In Edinburgh in 1831"... a sedate and civilized society routinely goes about its daily business, secure that reality is

precisely as it is usually perceived. This serene atmosphere works to ironic effect as well... by establishing a normalcy out of which the fantastic might later more strikingly emerge... Beneath this richly detailed surface... there stirs a world of frustration at the limits of human knowledge, of pain both treated and caused by doctors of the day, and of murder for hire—although commissioned for the best of reasons.... The film thus generates a tension between these first everyday images of civilization and the darker, blind depths which work upon it and with which it often unwittingly strikes a deal.[6]

The film begins with the company's trademark "global broadcasting tower," as it transmits the familiar announcement of "An RKO Radio Picture." The opening credits, accompanied by Roy Webb's main theme (with a melody in the style of a Scottish *pibroch*) are superim-

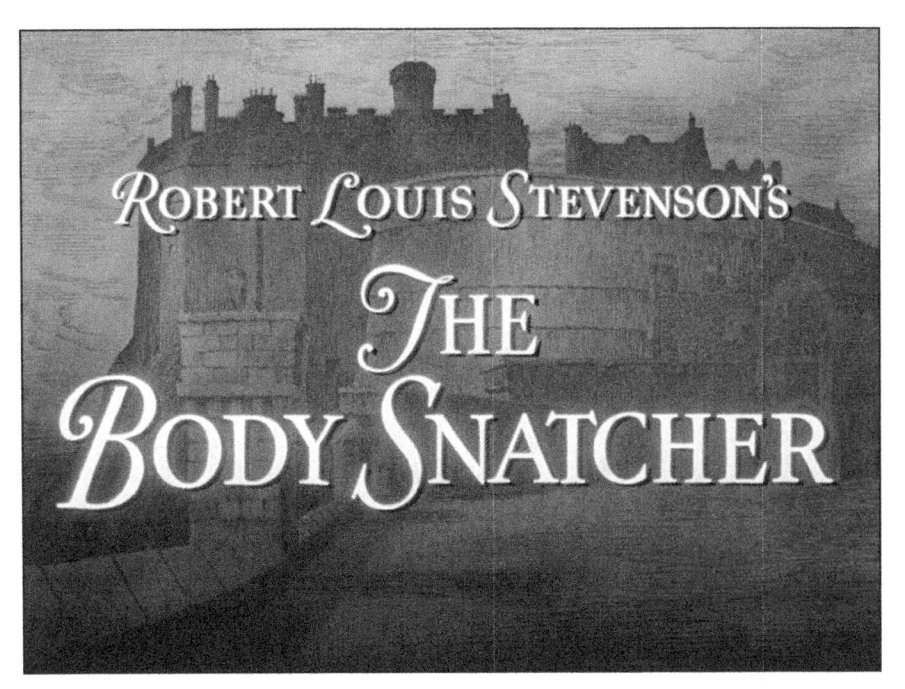

The Body Snatcher main title, superimposing Stevenson's name over a graphic of Edinburgh Castle.

posed over a graphic of Edinburgh Castle, which dissolves to actual footage of the site, shot atop the Castle Rock. As an open carriage drawn by a single horse heads away from the castle toward the right side of the frame, the stock image dissolves to a shot filmed at the RKO ranch, depicting a small carriage, drawn by two horses, moving down the street in front of the Street Singer and other inhabitants of the Old Town. The scene cuts to a medium shot of the singer with her busker's bowl. As she receives a donation, a dissolve leads to two more stock shots, including the royal palace of Holyroodhouse: the first showing a kilted Scotsman walking through an iron-gated entryway; and the second, a pair of shepherds driving a flock of sheep down the street toward a large pillared entrance.

Dissolving to the Greyfriars Kirkyard set, the initial dialogue scene features Fettes, framed in long shot, through an iron gate, as he sits atop a "mortsafe" grave monument, attempting to share his lunch with "Little Robbie," the Cairn terrier. Intent on guarding the

Stevenson is billed twice in the opening credits, here atop the Castle and above Philip MacDonald and Carlos Keith (Val Lewton).

Dissecting *The Body Snatcher* • 111

The graphic of Edinburgh Castle dissolves to this period footage filmed atop the Castle Rock.

The first appearance of the Street Singer (Donna Lee).

112 • *The Body Snatcher and the Making of a Horror Film Classic*

In this period shot of Edinburgh, a kilted Scotsman walks around the palace and into an iron-gated entryway.

The third period shot of Edinburgh features a pair of shepherds driving a flock of sheep down the street.

adjacent grave, the dog will accept food only from the hand of Mrs. McBride.

Introduced in long shot, as his coach moves along the street in front of Greyfriars to deliver a patient to MacFarlane's home, Gray is depicted as a complex character. Telotte notes, "Gray's coach subsequently serves as a visual link between the introduction of Fettes and that of MacFarlane, while it also hints at just how much generally goes hidden in this world."[7]

Holding Georgina Marsh, the disabled girl, in his arms, the grandfatherly cabman acquaints her with his horse while simultaneously appearing sinister when noticed at the door by MacFarlane's "secret bride," Meg Cameron. This moral ambiguity is a part of the literary Gray (since he does appear "evil" in life but ultimately "punishes" other evildoers after he dies), a quality wisely stressed by Lewton and Mac-

Fettes (Russell Wade), "Robbie" (Rex) and Mrs. McBride (Mary Gordon) in Greyfriars Kirkyard (scene still).

Cabman John Gray (Boris Karloff) passes Greyfriars Kirk.

Donald's writing and the alternately powerful and subtle direction of Wise.

When entering MacFarlane's house, mother and daughter are photographed from a high angle by De Grasse, whose camera is placed atop the large staircase leading to the second floor. After Meg leaves the room, the scene cuts to a low-angle shot, showing the imposing staircase looming over them in the background and, as the door opens to McFarlane's study, his shadow passing over them.

MacFarlane appears amiable at the outset, but soon proves stern and impatient. When Georgina refuses to describe her affliction, the doctor quickly concludes, "It's *useless*, Ma'am!" turning his back on them. Accused of stubbornness by Mrs. Marsh, Georgina whispers, "Mother, he *frightens* me."

Fettes arrives and, while taking "a chance to test [his] bedside manner," the girl warms up instantly. As the medical student carries her into the examination room, MacFarlane observes, "The child seems to take to the lad."

Dissecting *The Body Snatcher* • 115

Georgina Marsh (Sharyn Moffett) and Gray (Boris Karloff) arrive at Dr. MacFarlane's home and medical school. Mrs. Marsh (Rita Corday) stands in the background.

Gray (Boris Karloff) at Dr. MacFarlane's door (scene still).

Georgina (Sharyn Moffett) and Mrs. Marsh (Rita Corday) in MacFarlane's parlor.

Diagnosing a traumatic tumor on her spine, the doctor, sorely lacking in his own bedside manner, first raises the widow's hopes by announcing, "A very delicate operation—an operation which has never been performed before, but I believe it could be done," then insists he is not the man for the job.

"But doctor," pleads Mrs, Marsh, "in Leiden, in Paris, wherever I've taken Georgina, they've mentioned your name. I've come to think of you as our only hope." (In 1831, Leiden, Netherlands, was on par with Edinburgh as one of Europe's foremost centers of anatomical study.)

"Believe me, Madame, if I were only a doctor, I'd undertake this operation at once," explains MacFarlane. "But I'm more domini than doctor. I have a school to run... I have the responsibility of training thirty other doctors, to attend a thousand children like your own.... I am not heartless, Madame. I have every sympathy for you and the little girl, but if I were to consent to every operation brought to me, I'd have no time for teaching." Taking Mrs. Marsh by the arm, he leads her toward the door, adding, "And that's a great responsibility upon me, Ma'am. A *great responsibility*."

Dissecting *The Body Snatcher* • 117

Georgina (Sharyn Moffett) is frightened by Dr. MacFarlane.

MacFarlane (Henry Daniell) is frustrated by Georgina's silence:
"Oh, it's useless, Ma'am."

Fettes threatens to "give up med'cine... You see, my father is vicar at Thrums. It's a small parish, not much of a living..." This dialogue refers, not to Stevenson's story, but to literary works by his contemporary countryman J. M. Barrie, who created the fictional Scottish village of Thrums (from *thrums*, a weaving term referring to bits of unwoven yarn remaining in a loom after the cloth is removed), based on his own birthplace of Kirriemuir, Angus. Barrie used the setting in three novels, *Auld Licht Idylls* (1888), *Window in Thrums* (1889) and *The Little Minister* (1891).

Informing the lad from Thrums that he is "too good a man," Mac-Farlane insists, "I'll not let you quit." To insure compliance, he makes Fettes his assistant, which will provide for his "keep and... tuition, too," before escorting him to the anatomy room.

Bela Lugosi makes his entrance shortly after the 11-minute mark, enacting Joseph eavesdropping on MacFarlane and Fettes as they enter the laboratory, where he then pretends to be scrubbing a table. Sug-

Fettes (Russell Wade) meets Georgina (Sharyn Moffet): "Would you mind very much if I lifted you onto that table in there?"

Dr. MacFarlane (Henry Daniell) appoints Fettes (Russell Wade) as his new assistant.

gesting that the janitor might be "spying" on him, MacFarlane leads Fettes into the curtained-off back room, explaining that, because of "the law," there is a shortage of "bodies for dissection," prompting a dissolve to Greyfriars in the dead of night.

De Grasse's camera tracks into a close-up of the grave-watching "Little Robbie" as the clop-clop sound of a horse's hooves is heard in the near distance. A rusty gate latch squeaks open as the shadow of the body-snatcher, top-hatted, with spade and mattock resting on his shoulder, moves along the kirkyard wall. In this "resurrection" sequence, Gray performs the action many viewers consider his most heinous: the spade murder of the terrier, prior to digging up the corpse of Mrs. McBride's beloved son. (Bailey Fesler and Terry Kellum's audio of the spade hitting the grave, offsetting Roy Webb's sullen music, is jarring.)

The echoing thump of Gray's rapping on the laboratory door rouses Fettes to provide entry for the bodybag-toting cabman. Hitching the corpse a bit upon his shoulder with a grin, Gray walks into the

Joseph (Bela Lugosi), anatomy school servant and eavesdropper.

anatomy room. "Here, give me a hand. This is *heavy*," he informs the new assistant, adding, "You'll find the specimen in *good* condition." In a fine example of Lewton's poetical "Stevensonian" dialogue, the body-snatcher then describes his delivery: "He's as bright and lively as a thrush not a week long gone." When Gray queries his identity, the lad answers, "I—I'm Donald Fettes" (a line delivered with splendid innocence by Russell Wade). Mentioning recompense, Fettes learns that the cabman is quite an industrious fellow. "Of course, that's the sole of the business—for *pay*," Gray assures him. (Karloff exercises his sepulchral tones with delectable emphasis on the line, "I've no doubt that you have the key in your pocket—and the desk is *over there*.")

At the desk, Gray, turning up his palm toward Fettes, offers some advice (working in another dialogue reference to literature set in Scotland, Shakespeare's *The Tragedy of MacBeth*): "My fee is, as usual, ten pounds. Now, although it's none of my business, I'd make the proper entry, if I were you. Received—one specimen. Ten pounds, received from, shall we say, a Macduff? A *royal* name." As the Scots melody

Dissecting *The Body Snatcher* • 121

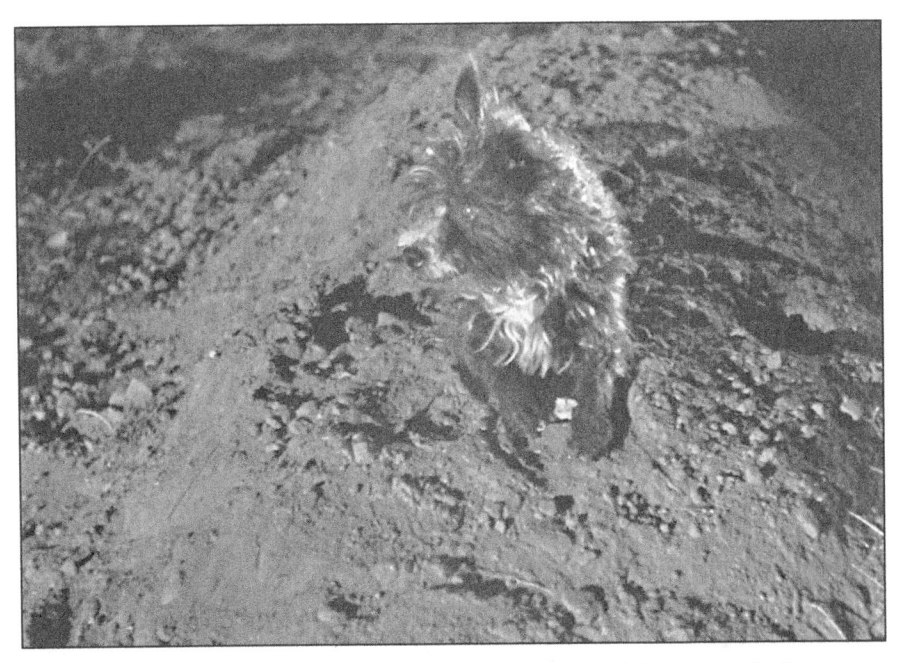

"Little Robbie" (Rex) is alerted by the sound of a horse's hooves and whinny.

Gray (Boris Karloff) enters Greyfrairs, his shadow cast across a "mortsafe" grave and along the kirkyard wall.

Hitching the corpse a bit upon his shoulder with a grin, Gray (Boris Karloff) prepares to enter MacFarlane's laboratory.

Gray (Boris Karloff) becomes acquainted with Fettes (Russell Wade).

in Webb's main theme punctuates the scene, Gray takes his leave with "My respects, Master Fettes. And may this be the first of many *profitable* meetings."

In this scene, Karloff begins the near-musical phrasing of his dialogue that he sustains throughout the film. (He does *sing* some of his dialogue in a later sequence.) It is a mesmerizing, yet admirably controlled performance, perhaps closer to Ardath Bey in *The Mummy* (1932) than to the more palpable bravura of his near-magical turn as the Monster in *Bride of Frankenstein* (1935) and dual characterization as Gregor and Anton de Berghman in *The Black Room* (1935). (He recently had completed his multiple year Broadway run, and the experience proved beneficial in more ways than one. *The Body Snatcher* provided the "quality" cinematic project he needed to transfer his growth as an actor from stage to screen. Or as Karloff explained it, Lewton was "the man who rescued me from the living dead and restored my soul."[8])

"My fee is, as usual, ten pounds," Gray (Boris Karloff) informs Fettes (Russell Wade).

Gray's closing of the anatomy-room door prompts a chuckle from MacFarlane, who, from the staircase, has been observing the conversation. "Well, well, my boy. Your first meeting with the redoubtable Gray. You can count it a milestone in your medical career."

The next morning, Fettes prepares to discuss some of Dr. Mac-Farlane's main points in anatomy class. Survis (Bill Williams), who has rigged a demonstration skeleton as a pugilistic practical joke, incites laughter among the other students. Fettes' irritation is short-lived, however, as Joseph interrupts to announce the arrival of "a lady." (Lugosi's one-line contribution to this sequence, culminating with a shrug, lasts eight seconds.)

Mrs. Marsh, fearing the progressive nature of Georgina's affliction will lead to paralysis, asks Fettes, "a kind man," to intercede with Mac-Farlane on their behalf. Back downstairs, he walks in on the doctor's

Joseph (Bela Lugosi) interrupts Fettes (Russell Wade): "A lady to see you" (scene still).

"Life can't be all skittles and ladies," Dr. MacFarlane (Henry Daniell) informs Fettes (Russell Wade) as Survis (Bill Williams, third from right) looks on.

edifying and entertaining anatomy demonstration: "In an adult, this muscle can apply more than 175 pounds of pressure. Double that, and you have the full strength of the human jaw. That, gentleman, is to chew our food and *bite our enemies*."

"Here, Fettes," MacFarlane declares as his assistant's footsteps on the stairs interrupt the students' laughter. "Life can't be all *skittles and ladies*. Well, I see it's time for our luncheon. I have a bit of *beef* to discuss—so I leave you to whatever arrangements you've made to serve the inner man." (The doctor's dialogue, written by Lewton, treads closely to Stevenson's own remark in his gloomy August 23, 1893, letter to Sidney Colvin: "Life is not all Beer and Skittles, and mine is closing in dark enough."[9])

Before leaving for lunch, MacFarlane confers about a subject's arm with Richardson (Robert Clarke), who incurs his wrath when joking, "Burke and Hare could never have got the best of him."

"It's a poor subject for jest—particularly for a medical student," scolds MacFarlane, ascending the stairs.

Dr. MacFarlane (Henry Daniell) reminds Richardson (Robert Clarke) that Burke and Hare make "a poor subject for jest."

"What did you say to his imperial highness?" asks Gilchrist (Carl Kent).

"Nothing but a merry word about Burke and Hare," Richardson replies.

"There's nothing in that to get excited about," says Gilchrist, naïvely. "They're dead and buried." (In 1831, Burke was dead, but his remains were still above ground, in the Edinburgh Medical Museum. As for Hare, having been escorted from Scotland, odds are even that he was still on terra firma, whereabouts unknown.)

Whistling a sprightly Scottish tune while walking toward his usual luncheon spot—Greyfriars—Fettes is surprised by a gathering, from which Mrs. McBride emerges tearfully to report, "They killed his wee doggie too— 'Little Robbie.'" Fettes returns to inform MacFarlane of the incident and his uncertainty about continuing at medical school.

Revealing the truth to Fettes, the doctor admits, "*I was an assistant once. I had to deal with men like Gray. Do you think I did it be-*

At Greyfriars, Fettes (Russell Wade) watches Mrs. Mary McBride (Mary Gordon) tearfully cradle the murdered Robbie: "They killed his wee doggie, too."

cause I wanted to? Do you think I want to do it *now*? But I *must*. And *you must*. Ignorant men have dammed the stream of medical progress with *stupid and unjust laws*. And if that dam will not break, the men of med'cine must find *other* courses.... I'm sorry for the woman, but her son might be alive today if more doctors had been given the opportunity to work with more human specimens. As for me, I let no man stop me when I know I'm right. When I know I need those lifeless subjects for my students' enlightenment and my own knowledge—and, if you're a *real man* and want to be a good doctor, you'll see it as I see it."

As MacFarlane and Fettes walk to Hobbs Public House, the Street Singer gives tongue to the first verse of "When Ye Gang Awa, Jamie":

> When ye *gang awa*, Jamie,
> Far across the sea, laddie.
> When ye *gang awa*, Jamie,
> What will ye send to me, laddie?

Dr. MacFarlane (Henry Daniell) is perplexed by Fettes' moral dilemma.

The Street Singer (Donna Lee) gives tongue to the first verse of "When Ye Gang Awa, Jamie."

Dissecting *The Body Snatcher* • 129

At Hobbs Public House, as Dr. MacFarlane (Henry Daniell) and Fettes (Russell Wade) enjoy the warmth of the fire, a familiar voice beckons, "A *fine specimen*, isn't he, 'Toddy?'"

Gray (Boris Karloff) extends an invitation MacFarlane cannot refuse: "Come, 'Toddy,' sit down here with me."

The art direction of Albert S. D'Agostino and Walter E. Keller, combined with the set decorations of Darrell Silvera and John Sturtevant, is most impressive in the Hobbs pub set, in which the high ceilings, ornate, dark wood, and alcoved bar give *The Body Snatcher* an authentic atmosphere of 1831 Edinburgh. De Grasse uses an "inside the fireplace" shot, showing doctor and student warming themselves as a boy sings and turns a spit, roasting a large pig. Off-camera, a voice beckons, "A *fine specimen*, isn't he, 'Toddy' MacFarlane? Come, 'Toddy,' sit down here with me."

Much of Stevenson's dialogue is reproduced in the film. In this scene, Lewton both lifted verbatim and expanded upon Gray's lone appearance in the story:

> One afternoon, when his day's work was over, Fettes dropped into a popular tavern and found Macfarlane sitting with a stranger. This was a small man, very pale and dark, with coal-black eyes. The cut of his features gave a promise of intellect and refinement which was but feebly realised in his manners, for he proved, upon a nearer acquaintance, coarse, vulgar, and stupid. He exercised, however, a very remarkable control over Macfarlane; issued orders like the Great Bashaw; became inflamed at the least discussion or delay, and commented rudely on the servility with which he was obeyed. This most offensive person took a fancy to Fettes on the spot, plied him with drinks, and honoured him with unusual confidences on his past career. If a tenth part of what he confessed were true, he was a very loathsome rogue; and the lad's vanity was tickled by the attention of so experienced a man.
>
> "I'm a pretty bad fellow myself," the stranger remarked, "but Macfarlane is the boy—Toddy Macfarlane, I call him. Toddy, order your friend another glass." Or it might be, "Toddy, you jump up and shut the door." "Toddy hates me," he said again. "Oh, yes, Toddy, you do!"
>
> "Don't you call me that confounded name," growled Macfarlane.

"Hear him! Did you ever see the lads play knife? He would like to do that all over my body," remarked the stranger.

"We medicals have a better way than that," said Fettes. "When we dislike a dead friend of ours, we dissect him."

Macfarlane looked up sharply, as though this jest was scarcely to his mind.

In the film, alone at his table, Gray is joined by both MacFarland and Fettes, the latter becoming captivated by the cabman's curious power and sarcastic charm. Prior to incorporating the material from Stevenson's story, Lewton features Gray using his influence to persuade MacFarlane to operate on Georgina.

MacFarlane:
I'm a teacher, not a practitioner.
Gray:
A teacher, eh? Maybe you're afraid to be a doctor.

Fettes (Russell Wade) observes the "influence" Gray exerts upon his mentor.

MacFarlane:
>Afraid—of what?

Gray:
>Afraid that you're not as good a doctor as you make out to be.

MacFarlane:
>I'm the best man for the job.

Gray:
>Why don't you do it, then? *I'd like* for you to do the operation, "Toddy."

MacFarlane:
>You—since when have you become the protector of little children?

Gray:
>It's not the child I'm concerned with, "Toddy." It's you I'm thinking of. I'd like to have you prove that a lot of things I know haven't hurt "Toddy" MacFarlane any.

MacFarlane:
>I'll not do it, Gray.

Gray:
>Oh, yes, you will. You'll do it to oblige Mr. Fettes and myself.

MacFarlane:
>No!

Gray:
>Maybe there's some private reasons between you and me that will make you. Some "long lost friends," eh, "Toddy?" *Say* you'll do it for me and Mr. Fettes here.

MacFarlane:
>It *might* be an interesting case.

Gray:
>*That's a good boy,* "Toddy!"

MacFarlane:
>You only want me to do it because I *don't want to. That's it,* isn't it, Gray?

Gray:
>"Toddy" hates me.

MacFarlane:
> *Don't* call me by that name.

Gray:
> (to Fettes) Hear him? Did you ever see the lads play knife? (He thrusts a knife into a loaf of bread.) Toddy would like to do that *all over my body.*

Fettes:
> We medicals have a better way than that. When we dislike a friend, we *dissect* him.

At this point, a meal is mentioned in the story, with Gray forcing MacFarlane to pay the bill. However, the cinematic cabman proclaims, "You'll never get rid of me *that way*, Toddy," a remark that becomes the verbal leitmotif for the remainder of the drama. "You and I have two bodies," Gray tells MacFarlane, "aye, very different sorts of bodies,

Dr. MacFarlane (Henry Daniell) objects to Gray (Boris Karloff),
"I will not have you call me by that name."

Gray (Boris Karloff) informs Dr. MacFarlane (Henry Daniell), "You'll never get rid of me that way, 'Toddy.'"

but they are closer than if we were in the same skin—for I saved that skin of yours once, and *you'll not forget it*."

Fading out on a perplexed Fettes, the narrative continues with the student's report to Mrs. Marsh on the "ramparts," where she is giving Georgina her "airing." He affirms that MacFarlane has given his "promise" to operate, but that "great pain and shock" will accompany the procedure. "*She's* brave enough, but I don't know about myself," replies the self-conflicted mother.

Fettes, in the Scots Presbyterian tradition, is indeed confident about the divinely ordained abilities of his mentor. When the widow admits, "Now that it seems so close, I wonder if I should dare trust my child into any but God's hands," he replies, "Dr. MacFarlane is a *great man*. I think he's the greatest man in med'cine. God would not have given him such gifts if they were not meant for Georgina's cure."

Georgina, thinking she hears "the white horse who's going to greet me when he sees me," asks to be taken to the wall overlooking the street below. Fettes is keen to oblige, but she disappointedly shakes her head. "It was a *brown horse*, Mommy." Fettes then cuts to the heart of the matter, realizing that her desire to have the animal "say hello" to her stems from "not hav[ing] friends enough."

"Of course, I don't *have friends*," the child admits. "That's because I can't walk. I try to make myself used to it, though."

Fettes counsels, "One shouldn't get used to the *wrong things*," before promising, "Dr. MacFarlane will make you well."

But the doctor is having problems of his own. Hungover from the previous evening's tipple with the wily cabman, he struggles to place a chunk of coal into the fireplace, finally sending carbon shrapnel flying across the room. Off-camera laughter announces the arrival of Meg, who asks rhetorically, "Gray's head. Is that it, 'Toddy'?" (MacFarlane doesn't mind being called *that name* by his wife.) Is that what you broke just now with the poker? Broken it, and have *done with him forever*."

Meg knows better, however. MacFarlane's inability to respond inspires her embrace. "My poor lad. My poor, poor lad that can never be free of him."

Fettes (Russell Wade) helps Georgina (Sharyn Moffett) look for the white horse.

Dr. MacFarlane (Henry Daniell) takes the fire poker to "Gray's head."

"You're *daft*," he finally replies. "What's Gray to me? He's only a *man*, from whom I buy what I need when I need it. The rest is forgotten."

Shaking her head, Meg pegs her husband, spot-on: "You may deny him, 'Toddy,' but you'll not rid yourself of him by saying the Devil is dead."

"Nonsense," he insists. "You're a *fey* creature, Meg, with *mad ideas*—but you have a wildness that holds you to me, my lass."

Referring to the class distinctions requiring her to pose as her husband's maid, she asks, "No *great lady* can ever take my place?"

Now MacFarlane shakes his head intently, before kissing her passionately—a move cut short by the *osculatus interruptus* of Fettes, who comes rapping at the door.

This dialogue and content written by Lewton is as impressive as that created for the scenes pairing MacFarlane with Gray. The writer-producer's development of this canny female (something that Stevenson was barred from doing by Victorian morality) is on par with that

Meg Cameron (Edith Atwater), canny Highlander and "secret wife," advises her husband, Dr. MacFarlane (Henry Daniell), "You may deny him, 'Toddy,' but you'll not rid yourself of him by saying the Devil is dead."

of the major male characters. As she explains to Fettes in a later scene, while MacFarlane may not realize the true, tragic nature of his association with the environment represented by the body-snatcher, *she* certainly does. Brilliantly, Lewton imbued Meg with enough depth, on a level even higher than the male "hero," Fettes, to depict her as the conscience of the film—a notable element in a "horror film" made in 1944.

"Some powders for that aching head?" MacFarlane inquires of Fettes. "That was a furious lot that we drank last night, and in *bad company*." Asked about "the operation," the doctor responds, "Fettes, you're a man of the world. You wouldn't hold me to a promise given in *drink*?" Told of the pledge given to Mrs. Marsh, he adds, "*Really*, Fettes, you irk me with your lack of understanding," following up with an excuse about the risk of performing an unsuccessful surgical procedure. "I'd have to study the matter ," he concludes. "Have we any subjects?"

Informed that the operation is "entirely out of the question," Fettes hang-doggedly exits MacFarlane's study. That evening, he heads toward Gray's lodgings, passing the Street Singer on the way. She again performs "When Ye Gang Awa, Jamie," this time the verse about "a silken gown wi' flounces *tae* the knee, lassie." Responding in the negative to his inquiry about the cabman, she still scores a coin in her busking bowl. His "Thank you, all the same" is met with more of the folk song.

Spotting a wooden shingle, marked "John Gray CABMAN" in white chalk, Fettes enters the building through a low door. De Grasse atmospherically shoots Wade from the back of the stable, behind a ladder and Gray's coach. Here, Lewton and Wise, via J. R. Whittredge's sharp editing, use a technique that came to be known as "the bus" (after an effective shot in *Cat People* involving a transit bus releasing its air brakes, making a panther-like sound which frightens both Alice Moore [Jane Randolph] and viewers of the film). As the scene cuts closer to Fettes, and De Grasse pans the camera rightward with him, the head of the white horse, accompanied by his loud snorting, suddenly enters the frame. After gently patting the animal's muzzle, Fettes then moves in the opposite direction, passing the coach as he slowly walks to knock on the door of Gray's room.

Trailed by his omnipresent cat, Gray, carrying a frying pan, strides (in the trademark Karloff gait) toward Fettes with an enthusiastic welcome. "Oh—the young doctor, come to see me. I'm honored—honored. *Come in.* Come in."

As Fettes prepares to sit in Gray's "most comfortable chair," the cat characteristically walks between his legs, brushing against the material of his woollen trousers. (The costumes by Renié are another effective period element.) In a tip of the bottle to Burke and Hare, Gray pours his guest some brandy. Accepting the libation, the anxious assistant inquires about "the chances of getting us a subject."

"Oh—that'd be difficult. *Very* difficult," Gray replies. "There was a dog that bothered me during the last job. People are so concerned about—*dogs*." The considerable silent pause Karloff inserts between "about" and "dogs" is a highpoint of his performance, and a simple but notable example of his nonverbal acting prowess (made even more effective by the absence of music in the scene). Noting that "the kirk-

Dissecting *The Body Snatcher* • 139

Fettes (Russell Wade) drops a donation into the Street Singer's (Donna Lee) busking bowl.

Fettes (Russell Wade) locates Gray's austere lodgings.

Fettes (Russell Wade) enters the humble habitation of Cabman John Gray.

Gray (Boris Karloff) characteristically offers a spot of brandy to Fettes (Russell Wade) (scene still).

yards are to be guarded," he foreshadows a future action by admitting, "I wouldn't want to say it'd be *impossible* to get a subject."

Fettes' palpable impatience strengthens Gray's resolve to control MacFarlane. "You may tell 'Toddy' that I'll do what I can, when I can, 'cause he knows I will." Turning on the Karloff malevolence, he points at Fettes, adding, "But he must wait and see, *like the children do*."

Perhaps emboldened by his wee nip of brandy, Fettes betrays his rising anger as he slams down the glass and heads back toward the stable. Gray does *not* wait to strike, however: As the sound of the Street Singer, vocalizing Lady Nairne's "Will Ye No Cam Back Again?" wafts in through the small door that looks onto the alley, he grasps the wooden frame, getting a glimpse of the girl, carrying her bowl and repeating the song's ironic title. A shot from behind Gray cuts to a medium close-up of him gazing out the door. Then De Grasse tracks in on Gray's face as Karloff turns his head, serpent-like, slightly toward

Gray (Boris Karloff) is ever mindful of public opinion: "People are so concerned about—*dogs*."

Gray's (Boris Karloff) intentions turn nefarious as he eyes the Street Singer.

his right shoulder, narrows his eyes, and then (in a bit of sublime nonverbal acting) widens *only* the left one. Closing the door, he informs the horse, "There's bad news, boy—bad news." Handing him a mouthful of hay, he adds, "We have to go out again."

The subsequent minimalist scene is illustrative of the "less is more" aesthetic approach favored by Val Lewton and Boris Karloff, both of whom spoke of their preference for the "power of suggestion" over more graphic depictions of violence in literature and cinema ("terror" rather than "horror"). The lone, static long shot of the Street Singer, uninterrupted by editing or musical scoring, begins with a return to her signature number, "When Ye Gang Awa, Jamie." As she passes under the stone arch, singing, "I'll send ye a *braw* new gown, Jeanie," the hooves of Gray's horse are heard on the soundtrack just before the animal's head enters the left side of the frame. Perched atop the coach, Gray, sparing the whip, steadily drives the horse closer behind the girl, who completes the verse:

> The *brawest* in a' the *toon*, lassie,
> And it shall be o'silk and *gowd*,
> Wi' Valenciennes set round, lassie.

The singer and coach both vanish into the darkness under the archway. Her voice is heard beginning the next verse of the song,

> That's *nae* gift *ava*, Jamie,
> Silk and *gowd* and a'—

The next word, "laddie," never comes—as her sustained note on "a'—" is followed by a chillingly abrupt sound of distress. The entire action of the scene, although precisely timed, is thoroughly believable.

Showing nothing of the resulting action, Lewton, Wise and De Grasse *tell everything*. This one-shot scene is one of Hollywood's most glorious moments of what French film theorist André Bazin called

Gray's (Boris Karloff) fatal pursuit of the Street Singer (Donna Lee), depicted in a single shot, is one of Hollywood's most glorious moments of "pure cinema."

"pure cinema." Arguably, this scene, elegant *storytelling* entirely dependent on blocking, lighting and the creative use of sound in the *mise-en-scène*, constructed in any other way, would suffer by comparison. (In the world of modern commercial filmmaking, with its movement away from *mise-en-scène* to style-driven manipulation of images—continuous (often gratuitous) camera movement, excessive editing and overmixed, unrealistic sound effects—such a strategy borders on the alien.)

The following scene, opening with Fettes studying in his room at MacFarlane's, also benefits from an absence of musical scoring. As they had receded into the distance in the previous scene, here the hooves of Gray's horse can be heard advancing toward the house, prompting Fettes to rise, open the window, and observe the resurrection man-turned-murderer arriving with his shouldered bundle.

Gray's burden appears lighter this time, as he enters the anatomy room effortlessly, grinning as he goes. "There, Master Fettes," he an-

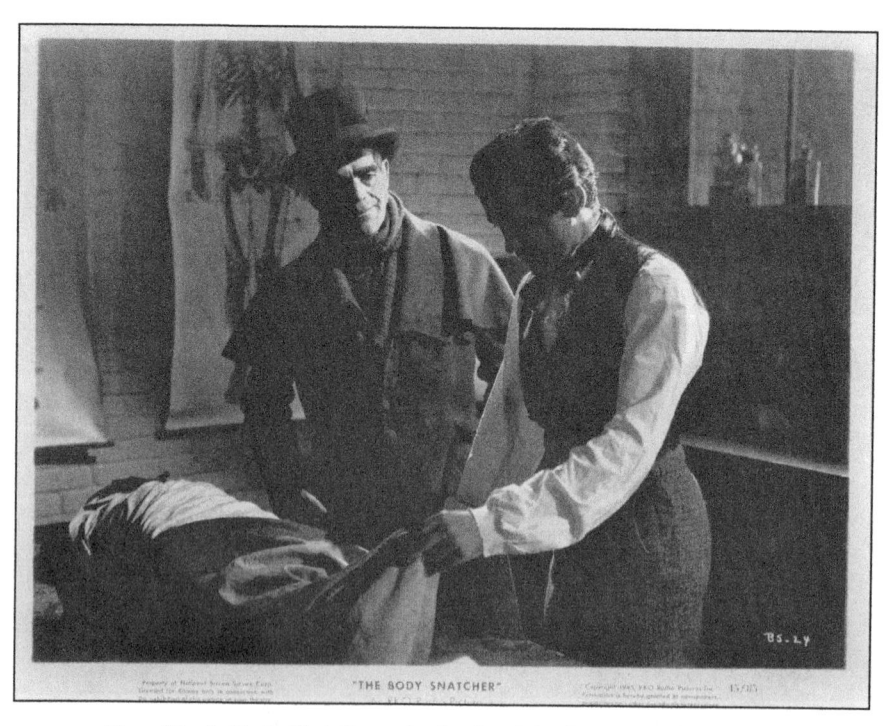

Gray (Boris Karloff) delivers the body of the "wild lassie from the Highlands" to Fettes (Russell Wade) (scene still).

Fettes (Russell Wade) realizes, "Why, that's the Street Singer."

nounces after the bundle is deposited on the laboratory table. "Sooner than we thought—a stroke of luck, you might say."

Fettes smiles, too, until he lifts the shroud to examine the face of the deceased. "Why, that's the Street Singer," he realizes. "I know her, I tell you. She was alive and hearty only this evening. It's *impossible* she can be dead. *You could not have gotten this body fairly.*"

Gray's grin has metamorphosed into a mild grimace (coupled with the intense Karloff eyes, staring daggers at Wade). "You're *entirely mistaken*," he counters. "You'd better give me my money and make the proper entry." Wresting the £10 from the assistant's hand, he regains his smile, stating sarcastically, "Goodnight, *Doctor* Fettes." Following his departure, Fettes again lifts the shroud from the corpse, as a violin reprising the first seven notes of "When Ye Gang Awa, Jamie" and the clop-clop of the horse's hooves are commingled on the soundtrack.

In the morning, MacFarlane, happily whistling himself down the laboratory stairs, is surprised by Fettes' news about the "beautiful… wild lassie from the Highlands," the "Street Singer who sang

MacFarlane (Henry Daniell) is informed by Fettes (Russell Wade), "This is *murder!*"

'When Ye Gang Awa, Jamie.'" While Fettes describes the previous evening's encounters with Gray, Joseph, forever creeping about, listens from outside a curtained entrance. "I mean to report it," vows Fettes. "It's like Burke and Hare all over again."

"I wouldn't do that. I wouldn't report it," MacFarlane advises.

"Graverobbing is one thing. This is *murder!*" Fettes insists.

As Joseph brews thoughts of blackmail, MacFarlane argues, "I don't know that. Neither do you." Again, the doctor's denial is followed by rationalization: "This subject may have been an epileptic: thrown a fit, fallen out of bed, cracked her skull and killed herself. There's everything explained."

Fettes refuses to accept such an account, even from MacFarlane, who instructs, "Believe it or not, it's best that you pretend that you do. After all, you ordered this subject. You received it here and paid for it. That makes you a party to murder, if it *was* murder." (As Daniell delivers his lines, Terry Kellum's re-recording of Donna Lee's "Jamie" vocal, processed with reverberation, echoes hauntingly on the soundtrack.)

Dissecting *The Body Snatcher* • 147

"But I didn't ask him to *kill*," Fettes emphasizes.

"Who would believe that?" the doctor speculates. "And then, someone else might recognize her. She was as well known as the Castle Rock. No—I think we should do what we always do: dissection. I'll help you, of course. I want the whole centrum for myself—the spinal work. You *know why*."

Anxious for MacFarlane to help Georgina and her mother, the assistant finally capitulates. The cinematic Fettes is neither, in Stevenson's terms, "lion" nor "lamb," but a medical student wrestling with a moral dilemma triggered by circumstances beyond his control. He feels personally responsible when Gray delivers the body of the Street Singer. (In the story, the men "with Irish voices" bring the girl's body without being commissioned.) Although he later becomes hardened toward the murders, Stevenson's Fettes does experience a brief tinge of remorse. For the film, Lewton merged the two graverobbers into the character of Gray, but the following passage is faithfully reproduced:

Joseph (Bela Lugosi) brews thoughts of blackmail.

"I know her, I tell you," he continued. "She was alive and hearty yesterday. It's impossible she can be dead; it's impossible you should have got this body fairly."

"Sure, sir, you're mistaken entirely," said one of the men.

But the other looked Fettes darkly in the eyes, and demanded the money on the spot.

This episode is Stevenson's version of the Mary Paterson murder. Lewton, in turn, based the cinematic Fettes on David Paterson and other Knox students.

MacFarlane's surgery on Georgina's spine occurs exactly at the film's midpoint. The scene fades in on a close-up of her wheelchair, the tartan plaid cushion being its only occupant. De Grasse pans the

During Dr. MacFarlane's operation on Georgina, Meg (Edith Atwater) offers a cup of tea to the anxious Mrs. Marsh (Rita Corday) (scene still).

"Bravo," Richardson (Robert Clarke, seated center) tells Dr. MacFarlane (Henry Daniell), as Fettes (Russell Wade, left), Survis (Bill Williams, standing center) and Gilchrist (Carl Kent, seated right) observe the surgery on Georgina's spine.

camera rightward to Meg pouring a cup of tea and attempting to hand it to the anxious Mrs. Marsh, who is seated on the divan in the waiting room. In the small operating "theater," the students observe as MacFarlane, assisted by Fettes and Richardson, cuts to "the heart of the matter." When the child lapses into unconsciousness, it is for "the better." The "final step... push[ing] the ganglia to one side" prior to making a single incision, renders the 20-minute procedure "done." "The repair is affected," announces MacFarlane. "Nothing left to do but replace the tissue, and let nature heal what is no longer a defect, merely a *wound*."

"Bravo," applauds Richardson. Completing his task, the doctor turns the patient over to Fettes' care.

Later, while studying in the laboratory, MacFarlane is interrupted by Joseph. "What the devil's the matter with you?" he asks sternly. "*What do you want?*"

Joseph (Bela Lugosi) announces Gray's (Boris Karloff) arrival to Dr. MacFarlane (Henry Daniell).

Boris Karloff, Bela Lugosi and Henry Daniell, captured by the stills photographer in a blocking strategy that differs from Robert De Grasse's shot in the film (scene still).

"Mr. Gray wants..." But before the "creeping" servant can finish his sentence, the doctor, stress ever-mounting, cuts him off. "I don't wish to speak to Mr. Gray! Tell him there'll be no more business between us."

From behind MacFarlane comes the ominous voice of Gray. "Good afternoon, 'Toddy.'" Realizing the cabman again has him cornered, the doctor dismisses the servant.

"Now, that wasn't a *friendly* thing I heard, 'Toddy,' not at all friendly," Gray protests, but MacFarlane reveals his new program involving "more lecturing and less dissection."

Gray notes "the end of business" between them, adding, "But we'll still be *friends*, 'Toddy.' I'll be stopping by once in a while to see you and Meg—'for *auld lang syne*.'" (Here, Lewton adds Robert Burns to his list of Scottish literary lions.)

"I suppose I can't prevent that," admits MacFarlane, 'for *auld lang syne*.'"

Gray (Boris Karloff) reminds Dr. McFarlane, "Do you think you're getting rid of me, 'Toddy?'"

Gray (Boris Karloff) is confronted by Joseph (Bela Lugosi).

Starting for the door, Gray turns back toward MacFarlane. "And do you think you're getting rid of me, 'Toddy?'" he reminds him, building a chuckle into a full-blown laugh as he takes his leave.

Heading for his hansom, Gray is blocked by Joseph, who requests a meeting. "Well, I presume you shall," Gray agrees, still chuckling. "This won't be my *last* visit here."

"I want to speak to you *alone*," insists Joseph. "I saw something—I heard."

Gray's query for more information is disrupted by the arrival of Fettes. "You'll have ample opportunity—*ample*," he declares as Joseph quickly walks off. Pivoting toward the house, Gray greets the assistant: "Good afternoon, *Master Fettes*."

Fettes, having just left Mrs. Marsh, reports that Georgina's "incision has healed, clean and fine, but she doesn't seem to have any desire to walk."

"As soon as she's ready," says MacFarlane, now confident in his abilities, "you bring her to me. *I'll* show her." Asked if he realizes "what happiness [he's] brought to those people," he replies, "That's the way of it, Fettes. You bring the lassie to me."

"Don't you want to find the white horse, Georgina?" the voice of Fettes inquires as the next scene fades in on a tight close-up of the agitated girl. "You can't find him from a wheelchair. You have to walk and run to find him."

Upon claiming she can't move her legs, MacFarlane forcefully interjects, "You can't! You can't! *Stop* trying to bribe her with childishness about white horses. Let her stand up and *walk*! Her spine's all right. I know it's all right!"

Fettes fires back: "But she must *want* to stand! She must *want* to walk!"

His anger boiling over, MacFarlane betrays his own sense of inadequacy as a doctor. "Can *I help it* if the child's a cripple? Of course, she wants to walk!" As tears well in Georgina's eyes, he orders, "Child,

"Get up out of that chair and walk!" Dr. MacFarlane (Henry Daniell) orders Georgina (Sharyn Moffett) as Mrs. Marsh (Rita Corday) and Fettes (Russell Wade) offer moral support.

I say to you, 'Get up out of that chair *and walk!*'" Full-blown weeping moves him to his knees. On the carpet, he issues more specific instructions.

Georgina raises herself to a standing position, but "her legs just won't move!"

"Nonsense!" shouts MacFarlane. "They will! They will!"

Mrs. Marsh has heard and seen enough. "I'm sorry, Doctor MacFarlane. Georgina's a good child, a *brave* child. You saw how she behaved during the operation. If she says she can't move, *she can't move.*"

Insisting that "everything is in place," MacFarlane then begins digging a deeper hole: "Then all my surgery is no good. There's something wrong with the child, something I don't know, something I can't define, can't diagnose. I can do *nothing for her.*" Commanding Fettes to "see Mrs. Marsh home," he then takes the only sensible course left to him: "I'm going to Hobbs. You can join me there later, if you want."

A dissolve leads to a bartender drawing ale from a huge keg at the Hobbs pub. Setting down his pewter mug, Gray announces, "Well, I'll be off, unless you have a fare for me, some gentleman a little taken with his wine."

"MacFarlane will want to be freighted home," replies the barman. "He's in the other room, getting *stiffer than the bodies he demonstrates.*"

This time, Gray's utterance of "Toddy" is all that is needed to garner an invitation from MacFarlane, already well into his cups as he sits, head in hand, at a small table in a private alcove. His offer: "Have a glass with me" prompts the cabman to claim, "You're uncommon friendly tonight, 'Toddy,'" and declare the encounter "more like the *old* days."

"I want someone to talk to," MacFarlane admits. "That Fettes—all taken up with the widow—never came back here." As the cabman pours a libation for his "friend," the doctor asserts, "Gray—you know something about the human body."

As the scene cuts to a medium two-shot, Gray tips up the bottle and replies (in another delicious moment for Karloff, flashing a wee grin as he delivers the line), "I've had *some* experience."

"Then you can understand this," expounds MacFarlane, gesturing with his hands. "The backbone—here are a lot of little blocks, and

Gray (Boris Karloff) reminds MacFarlane (Henry Daniell) about his knowledge of the human body: "I've had *some* experience."

those blocks are all held together, so that it works—*works*, like that whip of yours. You know that, don't you?"

Relishing MacFarlane's condescension, Gray responds, "I've never had it all explained by so *learned* a man."

"*I* set those blocks together, patched the muscles, put the nerves where they should be. I did it, and I did it *right*." Dropping his head back into his left hand, MacFarlane concedes, "She *won't walk*."

"Oh," Gray realizes, taking a drink, "It's the bit of a girl Fettes was talking about."

"Look here, Gray," MacFarlane demonstrates, "I fitted them together, like this—" Placing the bowl of one brandy glass on top of another, he motivates Gray to halt his self-pity by dashing them to the floor.

Gray:
 You can't build life the way you put blocks together, Toddy.

MacFarlane:
> What the devil are you talking about? I'm an anatomist. I know the body. I know how it works.

Gray:
> You're a fool, Toddy, and no doctor. It's only the *dead ones* you know.

MacFarlane:
> I *am* a doctor. I teach med'cine.

Gray:
> Like Knox taught you? Like *I* taught you? In cellars? In graveyards? Did Knox teach you what makes the blood flow?

MacFarlane:
> The heart pumps it.

Gray:
> Did he tell you how thoughts come and how they go—and why things are remembered, and forgot?

MacFarlane:
> The nerve center—the brain.

Gray:
> What makes a thought start?

MacFarlane:
> The brain, I tell you—I know.

Gray:
> You *don't* know, and you'll *never* know or understand, "Toddy." Not from Knox or me would you learn those things.

With another reptilian dart of his head, Karloff commands, "Look—," as Gray turns MacFarlane toward a mirror hanging on the wall beside the table. The camera shifts to the "point of view" of the mirror, as De Grasse's evocative chiaroscuro lighting highlights Karloff's malevolent visage. Gray continues, "Look at yourself. Could you be a doctor, a *healing* man, with the things those eyes have seen? There's a lot of knowledge in those eyes, but no understanding. You'd not get that from me."

"I am a doctor, I tell you, a *good* doctor," MacFarlane maintains. "I could make her walk, but she *won't*. She *won't!*"

Gray (Boris Karloff) asks Dr. MacFarlane (Henry Daniell), "Do you think you can be a doctor, a *healing* man, with the things those eyes have seen?"

Dr. MacFarlane (Henry Daniell) asks, "What are you holding over me?" to which Gray (Boris Karloff) replies, "*I'll* tell you *what*."

"Here, have another glass, MacFarlane," Gray advises, pouring a dram. "Then I'll take you safely home, and we'll be friends again—now that you *know* you're Knox's man and *my friend—aye, forever.*"

"I'm my own man," MacFarlane contends. "And I'll have no more to do with you, Gray. Why should I be afraid of you? What are you holding over me?"

Blending elements from James Gray's testimony and William Hare's subsequent harassment by vigilante mobs in the 1829 murder case, the scene continues with the cabman serving up a stark reminder from the two characters' mutual past: "*I'll* tell you *what*. I stood up in the witness box and took what should have been coming to *you*. I ran through the streets, with the mud and the stones around my ears, and the mob, yelling for my blood because you were afraid to face it—yes, and you're *still afraid.*"

Gray (Boris Karloff) is ordered by Dr. MacFarlane (Henry Daniell) to "stay away from my house, my school, and *from me!*"

"No—I'm not afraid," claims MacFarlane. "*Tell. Shout* it from the housetops—but remember this: They hanged Burke. They mobbed Hare, but Doctor Knox is living like a gentleman in London."

Glancing from MacFarlane down to the tabletop, Gray acquiesces, "Aye, there's something in what you say, 'Toddy.'"

"There is *much* in what I say, Gray," asserts MacFarlane, rising to his feet, "and if you've any regard for your neck, you'll leave now, and stay away from my house, my school, and *from me!*"

"Well," acknowledges Gray, "I've no wish for a rope cravat." Reaching up and massaging his neck, he then grabs his top hat and whip. "I never liked the smell o' hemp, so I'll *bid you goodnight, Doctor MacFarlane.*"

Gray claims he is incapable of teaching "understanding" to MacFarlane, but he does so in this scene. He observes that the doctor has

Gray (Boris Karloff) tells his "old friend" (Henry Daniell), "I never liked the smell o' hemp, so I'll bid you goodnight, Doctor MacFarlane" (scene still).

the intellectual capacity required for medical technique but does *not* possess the human feeling to carry it out. Gray's talent for blackmail, combined with the doctor's dependence upon the cabman's "resurrection" abilities, does not allow MacFarlane an escape from his antagonistic alter ego.

While the doctor continues the drinking binge, the cabman returns to his lodgings. As he feeds his horse, a "guest" drops in unexpectedly. Startled by the slamming door, Gray pivots, coming face to face with Joseph. "Ah, Doctor MacFarlane's man—a *surprise* visit. Come in. Come in."

With Joseph installed in the comfortable chair, Gray takes his own, petting his cat as the interloper summons up the courage to ask, "Can anyone hear what we say?"

"Only 'Brother,'" Gray answers, glancing down at the content feline.

"I know you *kill* people—to sell bodies," Joseph reveals.

Gray maintains his straightforward stare. "You say you came here of your own account? No one sent you? No one knows that you are here?"

"Give me money," demands Joseph. "Or I tell the police you murdered the subjects."

Releasing the cat, Gray rises. "Well, Joseph, you shall *have* money. Why should you not?" Walking across the room, he fetches the bottle of brandy and two glasses. "I don't suppose the great Doctor MacFarlane is over-lavish with his pay, ah?" he asks, preparing to pour for his guest. "Here, have a glass of this." Gray barely sips while Joseph downs the water of life. Refreshing his glass, Gray repeats, "You want money, and you shall have it." Now he reaches toward the fireplace mantle. "Let me see." Pulling down a metal container, he begins counting out bills. "Five, and five—and then, in gold, six." Replacing the container and returning to his chair, he continues, "Shall we say sixteen pounds, Joseph?" handing the money to his desirous visitor.

"Yeah," Joseph mutters, seizing the beneficence. "I have made you give me money, but you smile. Aren't you angry?"

"*No*, Joseph," Gray assures him, pouring yet another dram. "Here's some more brandy. I'll wager it's better than the doctor's, eh?" elicit-

Dissecting *The Body Snatcher* • 161

Gray (Boris Karloff), petting "Brother," asks Joseph, "No one knows that you are here?"

Joseph (Bela Lugosi) demands, "Give me money—or I'll tell them that you murdered the subjects."

Joseph (Bela Lugosi) attempting to extort Gray, as captured by the stills photographer (scene still).

Gray (Boris Karloff) prepares to silence Joseph's threat.

Dissecting *The Body Snatcher* • 163

ing a laugh from Joseph. "Drink up, man, drink up!" As Joseph tips the glass, Gray, snapping his fingers, declares, "I have an idea, a *splendid* idea—so *excellent* an idea that we must drink on it." Pouring a double, he now adds a little flattery to his scheme: "You see, I admire you, Joseph. It took *courage* to come here, and I'm looking for such a man." As the increasingly befuddled extortionist continues imbibing the brandy, Gray tells him, "You and I should work *together*."

"You mean, we would sell the bodies to the doctors together—to *dig 'em up*?" Joseph asks.

"They'll be no digging," Gray replies. "The kirkyards are too well guarded." Inching closer to Joseph, he adds, "We will, so to speak, *burke* them."

"*Burke* them?" puzzles Joseph.

"You're lately come to Scotland?" asks Gray.

"Aye," he responds. "I come from Lisbon."

Accepting Gray's payment, Joseph asks, "Aren't you angry?"

Gray (Boris Karloff) pours Joseph (Bela Lugosi) another dram: "Here's some more brandy. I'll wager it's better than the doctor's, eh?"

At this point, Karloff performs a song incorporated by Lewton, resembling an actual quatrain made popular in the streets of Edinburgh by chapbook sellers and singers after 1829:

> Up the close and doon the stair,
> But and ben' wi' Burke and Hare.
> Burke's the butcher. Hare's the thief,
> Knox the boy that buys the beef.

In the film, Gray prefaces his vocal performance by explaining to Joseph, "But you may have heard the chapbook singers and peddlers of verse cry their names down the street. You know—"

> Gray (singing):
> The ruffian dogs, the Hellish pair.
> The villain Burke, the meager Hare.

Joseph:
>Never heard the song. What did they do?

Gray:
>Eighteen people they killed and sold the bodies to Dr. Knox. Ten pounds for a large, eight for a small. That's good business, Joseph!

Joseph:
>Uh—where did they get the people?

Gray:
>That was Hare's end. Ah, you should have seen him on the streets. When he saw some old beldame deep in drink, how he cozened her. "Good-day to you, Madame Tosspot! And would you like a little glass of something before you take your rest? Come with me to my house, and you shall be my guest. You shall have *quarts* to drink, if you like!" Ha, ha! How he cozened them!

Gray (Boris Karloff) demonstrates for Joseph (Bela Lugosi) the modus operandi of Burke and Hare: "Come with me, Madame Tosspot..."

Joseph:
> We can *do that*? But when we get them there—then what?

Gray (singing):
> Nor did they handle axe or knife,
> To take away their victim's life.
> No sooner done, than in the chest,
> They crammed their lately welcomed guest.

Joseph:
> I don't understand the song. Tell me plain how they did it.

Here, the scene cuts to a tight close-up of Gray, from the viewpoint of the intoxicated Joseph (hence Wise's decision to show Karloff's face slightly out of focus). "I'll *show* you how they did it, Joseph," Gray explains. "I'll show you how they *burked* them. No, put your hand down. How can I show you, man? This is how they did it, Joseph."

In several scenes, Karloff literally was able to integrate his own personality into the multifaceted Gray, exhibiting sincere gestures of kindness, even gentleness, toward Georgina and requesting that the indifferent MacFarlane perform the spinal operation. This personality trait also is suggested after he has smothered the inebriated Joseph. During an earlier conversation with Fettes, Gray is shown tenderly petting the cat (an interesting contrast to his previous killing of the dog). This image recurs, in more subtle form, as Joseph lies expired on the floor: In a moment of inspired direction and performance, Gray removes his hands from Joseph's mouth and gently reaches over to stroke the cat, allowing the animal's tail to slide slowly through his palm. The cat's moniker, "Brother," suggests the degree of Gray's identification with the animal, a cunning creature capable of stalking silently through the night. Wise later claimed that this act of psychological duality, simultaneously depicting Gray's murder of Joseph and love for the cat, "was Karloff's idea."[9]

The scene provides another example of the musical restraint maintained by Roy Webb, whose melodic leitmotif enters the mix only after Gray rises from the floor to grab a body bag from a nearby cabinet. As the Scottish theme continues on the soundtrack, with the "burking" of Joseph accomplished, Gray now awards himself with a brandy dram.

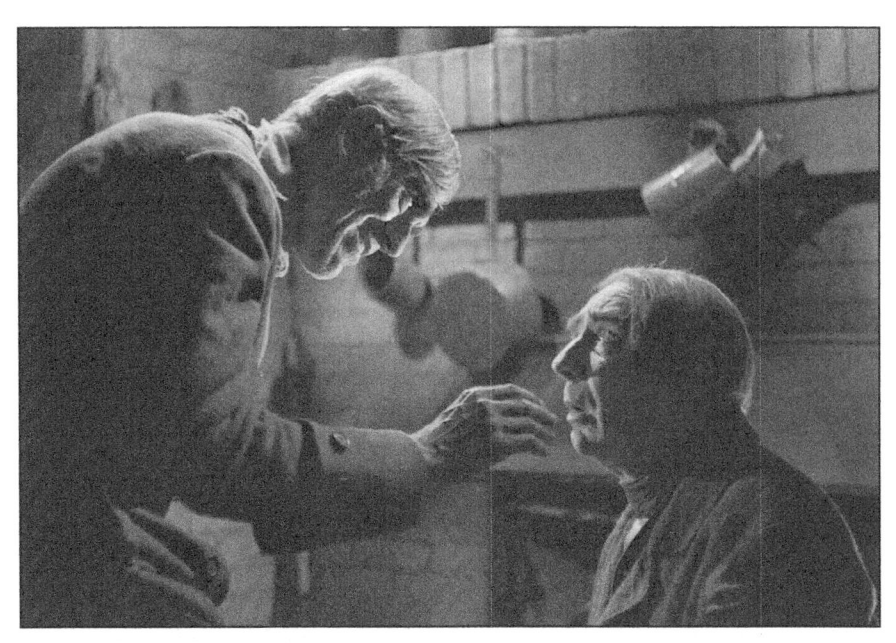

Gray's (Boris Karloff) demonstration for Joseph (Bela Lugosi) becomes a *fait accompli*: "I'll show you how they *burked* them."

Gray (Boris Karloff) about to "burke" Joseph (Bela Lugosi), from the perspective of the stills photographer (scene still).

Gray (Boris Karloff) administers the *coup de grace* to Joseph.

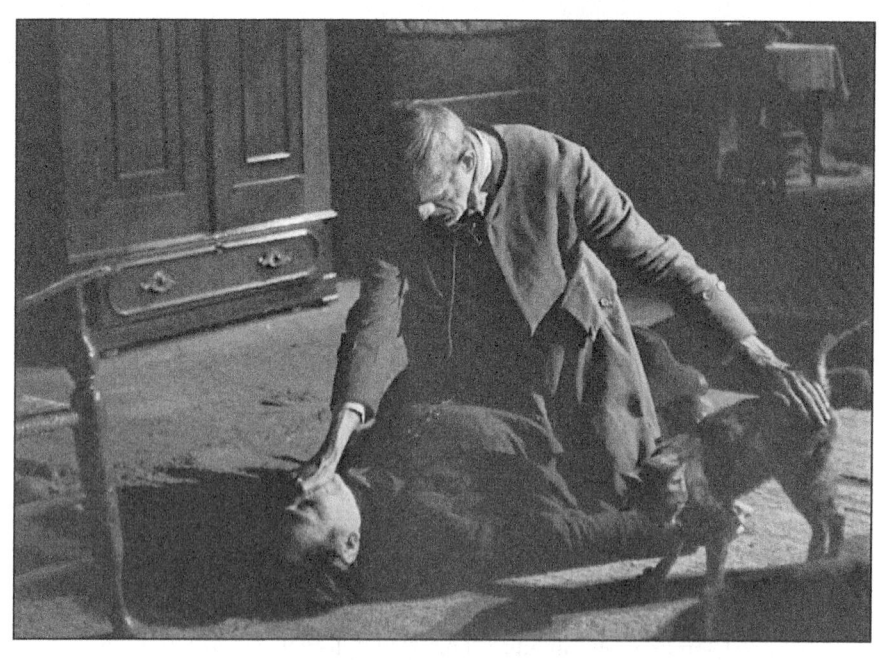

Gray (Boris Karloff) "burkes" Joseph and strokes "Brother."

Gray drives to MacFarlane's laboratory and, while toting Joseph's corpse into the back room, happily hums the melody to the "Burke and Hare" song he had just performed for his own "lately welcomed guest." As Lewton and Wise had done with the scene involving Gray's murder of the Street Singer, here they again display an admirably restrained approach, relying only on sound (Karloff's humming, tearing of the body bag, and splashing of the water as the corpse enters the brine vat), coupled with a slow forward tracking shot by De Grasse. The unedited shot, with the camera lingering on the curtain dividing the anatomy laboratory from the room where the "subjects" are stored, and ending when Gray re-emerges and climbs upstairs to visit his "crony," Meg, runs a total of 34 seconds.

Meg refers to Gray's company as "no good fortune," but when her "old friend" is remindful that *he* was responsible for introducing her to MacFarlane, she softens, inquiring, "Why must you be at him all the time?"

Gray (Boris Karloff) totes the corpse of his "lately welcomed guest" toward MacFarlane's brine vat.

Gray (Boris Karloff) tells Meg, "I like to see my friends. I like to visit 'em."

"He's *my friend*," Gray, holding a pewter tankard, replies. "I like to *see* my friends. I like to visit 'em." As he warms his left hand at the fireplace, the sound of the front door prompts Meg to hint at his impending departure. Entering the room, MacFarlane is surprised by the presence of the grinning, tippling cabman. Complaining about being begrudged a glass with his old crony, Gray is ordered out of the house, to which he responds, "I brought you a little present, MacFarlane, in very *good condition*."

MacFarlane neither ordered nor will accept anything from Gray, gift or otherwise. "You are *not* to set foot in this house again, for business or any other reason, and you're *getting out now!*" he loudly demands, grabbing Gray by the shoulders.

"I wouldn't do it," cautions the cabman. "I wouldn't be *heavy-handed*." As MacFarlane removes his hands, Gray adds, "It might become known that, when the great Doctor MacFarlane finds his anatomy school without subjects, he provides them *himself*, from *the midst of his own household*."

Gray (Boris Karloff) advises Dr. MacFarlane (Henry Daniell), "Take a look downstairs, 'Toddy.'"

"What the devil are you talking about?" asks MacFarlane.

"Take a look downstairs, 'Toddy,'" Gray grins before walking toward the door. Donning his top hat, he looks back, repeating, "*Take a look downstairs.*"

Discovery of Joseph in the brine vat is followed by MacFarlane's orders, "Fettes, the more things are wrong, the more one must act as if everything were right. You must do with Joseph as you did with the Street Singer: complete dissection and proper entry in the book."

Here, Fettes finally draws the line: "I'll not put my neck into a noose, not even for your sake, Doctor MacFarlane!"

"Don't be a fool, you can't begin and *then stop*," MacFarlane informs him, mentioning his handwritten log entry for the Street Singer. "You'll do as I say. As for me, I'll attend to Gray." Meg, who has been listening, attempts to stop him, but is pushed aside. "You must *leave me alone!*" commands MacFarlane.

Meg (Edith Atwater) observes Dr. MacFarlane (Henry Daniell) inform Fettes (Russell Wade), "You can't begin and *then stop!*"

Fettes tells "Mistress Cameron" that the anatomy room is "no place" for her, and that he "will help [her] upstairs, but she advises him to "leave this house." "Save yourself, Master Fettes," she explains. "Look at MacFarlane."

"But he's a great doctor—a *great man*," argues the assistant.

"A 'great man,'" repeats the doctor's secret bride. "Is it a great man whom Gray can order to his bidding? Is it a great man who, for very shame, dare not acknowledge his own wife? So that I must play maidservant, for the world's sake and his success. He could have been a great man, a *good* man and a *fine doctor*. But there was always the shame of the old ways and the old life to hold him back. And *Gray—* Gray, to hound him to his death."

"But Gray's only a resurrection man," counters Fettes, "who robs graves to make a little bit of money now and again."

"If he were only that," she disputes. "The man's *evil* himself. Someday you'll know him as MacFarlane knows him. For MacFarlane was to Knox as you are to him. That's how he met Gray, and worsted with him and drank with him. Aye, and Gray even brought him to my door—and my love. There's all that between them and more: Burke and Hare and Knox." Meg's revelation (superbly enacted by Edith Atwater), providing Fettes with the entire truthful history of the matter, reveals her deep understanding of her husband and his imminent fate. Assuming that Gray's threats of blackmail have run their course, Fettes is corrected further by the astute woman: "Gray has no need to threaten. Do you remember the trial?"

"I heard my parents speak of it in Thrums," Fettes replies. "It was a famous case."

"And do you remember the porter who testified against Burke?" she asks. "They didn't tell you how that porter cried out from the witness box, when the King's Councillor pressed him hard. How he cried

Meg (Edith Atwater) warns Fettes (Russell Wade) about MacFarlane and Gray: 'The pit yawns for them. I would have you away from them and safe out of the torment."

out that he was shielding a gentleman of consequence. That porter was *Gray*. And the gentleman of consequence who couldn't swallow the shame of it, who took my last paltry savings to hire Gray—"

"MacFarlane," realizes Fettes.

In *The Body Snatcher*, MacFarlane is primarily the healing agent, and Gray is seen as preying on both the living and the dead, but the distinctions are blurred consistently. The poor resurrection man Gray possesses a greater understanding of humanity than does the learned Dr. MacFarlane.

"Listen to me, Fettes," she entreats him, grabbing the lapels of his dressing gown. "I'm one part over heels in love with MacFarlane—and one part *fey*. You're a Lowlander, Fettes, and you have no way of knowing what we Highlanders call "The Second Sight.""

"I've heard of it," admits Fettes.

"It's *a gift* to my people. And I see MacFarlane and Gray. The pit *yawns* for them. I would have you away from them and safe out of the torment." Atwater builds her intelligent performance throughout the film, reaching a high point in this scene with a controlled intensity that stands alongside the efforts of her male counterparts (no easy task, considering the work contributed by Karloff and Daniell).

"Brother," the cat, is the first actor to appear in the next scene, in which Gray returns to his lodgings following a busy evening. Tossing his topcoat and hat aside, he walks to the fireplace to draw a flame with which he can light an adjacent wall candle. Rising from the fire, he throws the light from his taper on the back wall, where MacFarlane is seated in a wooden chair. His expression unaffected by this discovery, Gray lights the candle and finally responds, "This is unexpected, 'Toddy.'"

MacFarlane demands to know what Gray expects from him. "I want nothing of you, 'Toddy,'" claims the cabman, but the doctor insists, "*Gray*, I must be rid of you. You've become a cancer, a *malignant, evil cancer* rotting my mind."

"Then you've made a *disease* of me, eh, 'Toddy?'" scowls Gray.

"There's only one cure," he prescribes. "I must *cut you out*. I'll not leave here until I've finished with you, one way or another. I've got to be *sure* that I'm rid of you. And, if there's no other way—"

"Surely you're not threatening an *old friend*?" Gray inquires.

Gray (Boris Karloff) insists to Dr. MacFarlane (Henry Daniell), "I want nothing of you, 'Toddy.'"

MacFarlane again attempts to dispel the cabman's delusion: "We've *never* been friends."

Characteristically, Gray offers him "a drink of *something good*," but the medico reports "I've *drunk enough* tonight."

"Another little drop will never do you any harm" is his typical response.

"You're *getting old*, Gray, and it's a hard life driving a cab through these wet, windy streets of Edinburgh," MacFarlane claims.

"I have other means of sustenance," emphasizes Gray.

"*Resurrection* business? That may end sooner than you think. *New laws* may come." (Indeed, the Anatomy Act was passed by the House of Lords on July 19, 1832.) MacFarlane then makes his pitch: "Wouldn't you be more comfortable at Leith, in a neat little house?"

Gray looks genuinely pained. "Would you *bribe* me to let you be?"

"I'd make you rich," MacFarlane emphasizes, now taking a spot of brandy.

Rising to refresh the glass, Gray responds, "That wouldn't be half so much fun for me as to have you come here and *beg*."

"Beg?" retorts MacFarlane. "Beg of you, you *crawling graveyard rat*?"

"Aye," Gray whispers in response. "That is my pleasure."

"Very well then," MacFarlane capitulates. "I beg of you. I *beseech* you."

"And I would lose the fun of having you come back again," explains Gray.

"But, why, Gray, *why*?" demands the doctor.

"It would be a hurt to me to see you no more, 'Toddy.' You're a *pleasure* to me," he explains further.

"A pleasure to *torment* me?" probes MacFarlane, his agitation increasing.

"No," admits Gray, "a pride to know I can *force* you to my will. I am a *small* man, a *humble* man, and being poor, I have had to do

Gray (Boris Karloff) admits to Dr. MacFarlane (Henry Daniell),
"I am a *small* man, a *humble* man…"

Dissecting *The Body Snatcher* • 177

much that I did not want to do. But so long as the great Doctor Mac-Farlane jumps at my whistle, *that long am I a man*—and if I have *not that*, I have *nothing*. Then I am only a *cabman* and a *graverobber*."

Gray's next remark, his signature "You'll *never* get rid of me," sends MacFarlane over the edge. As Webb's score surges into a dominant position on the soundtrack, the two characters (here played by the two stuntmen) lunge murderously at each other after MacFarlane, a split second before Gray, makes the first move. In a film written, photographed, edited and directed so impressively, this sequence, combining the painfully obvious doubles for Karloff and Daniell with cutaway reaction shots of the cat, is the overall low point (and the opposite of the brilliant long-take scenes involving Gray's victims, the Street Singer and Joseph, that precede it). However, the inclusion of close-ups of Karloff (Gray warning, "Let be, 'Toddy.' *Let be*. I have no wish to hurt you," as he attempts to "burke" him) and Daniell (MacFarlane struggling under Gray's huge hand) help balance the scene. A

Gray (Boris Karloff) attempts to "burke" Dr. MacFarlane: "Let be, 'Toddy.' *Let be*."

two-shot of them struggling on the floor (in which MacFarlane feigns his suffocation) then brackets inserted close-ups of Karloff (Gray stating with relief, "That's better, 'Toddy'") and Daniell (Gray's voice continuing, "That's more reasonable").

The action shot of the stuntmen returns before Wise cuts to a shot of their shadows on the wall (where the cat is sitting atop a chest of drawers), culminating with one character smashing a chair over the head of the other and bludgeoning him with one of the wooden legs. The shadow of the living character hoists that of the dead one, and the scene dissolves to a mobile camera shot, progressing through MacFarlane's laboratory, and the sound of Gray's coach joining Webb's music on the soundtrack.

The top-hatted killer carrying his occupied body bag into the anatomy room is revealed to be "Toddy" MacFarlane, who asks Meg about the whereabouts of Fettes.

"He's gone," admits Meg. "I sent him away. I'll not see another

Meg (Edith Atwater) is advised by Dr. MacFarlane (Henry Daniell), "Take a look at the face."

boy made miserable like you, 'Toddy.'" Observing the body bag on the table, she deduces, "You've been with Gray."

"Aye," admits MacFarlane. "You'd better look at the face. Look at it, Meg." After she lifts the cloth, he announces, "I'm rid of him forever. He'll not come here again, sneaking and whining and bullying. Now, he'll serve a *good* purpose. And, tomorrow, when the last bit of him is dissected, demonstrated, and entered in the students' notebooks, then, at last, there's an *end* to him. Next day, I'll take his horse and cab to sell at Penicuik Fair. Then, *not a trace left. Rid of him, forever.*"

Turning to ascend the stairs, Meg stops to inform him, "No, 'Toddy,'" and as the scene cuts to a close-up of Atwater, "You're *not* rid of him."

As children run and play on the ramparts, Fettes bids good morning to Mrs. Marsh and Georgina, revealing that he has left the anatomy school. "I feel that I've learned nothing from MacFarlane," he admits. He taught me the mathematics of anatomy, but he couldn't teach me the poetry of med'cine."

Still seeking the white horse, Georgina (Sharyn Moffett) walks again.

Sitting by the wall, holding her doll, Georgina again hears the familiar sound of a horse's hooves. She cries out to her mother, who is preoccupied with Fettes' account. "I feel that MacFarlane had me on the wrong road—a road that led to knowledge, but not to healing. If there had been any healing in the man, Georgina would be walking now," he claims.

Again raising herself to a standing position, the girl cries out, "Mommy, it's the white horse. I'm *sure* it's the white horse!" Being ignored has its benefit, as she forces herself to take a step. Arriving at the stone barrier, she is still unable to peer over it. Finally noticing the child's successful struggle, the widow and former medical student rush to her side.

Quite optimistic, Fettes pushes away the wheelchair: "You'll not need that again, Georgina." Instinctively, he returns to tell MacFarlane the good news.

Meg (Edith Atwater) accedes to Fettes' (Russell Wade) request: "If you must babble your news to him, he's at the Fishermans Tryst, the inn at Penicuik" (scene still).

Reticent to divulge MacFarlane's whereabouts, Meg realizes, "There's no standing between a fool and his folly. If you must babble your news to him, he's at the Fishermans Tryst. It's the inn at Penicuik." Fettes, taking MacFarlane's horse and gig, dashes to the familiar locale.

At the Tryst, "Old Angus, the Horsestealer" (Jim Moran) is boasting to his mates about practically pilfering Gray's "sound horse and closed carriage" from MacFarlane for £4, 10s. At the behest of the barmaid, the horse trader ponies up a few token coins. "Piper, let's have a song!" one of the patrons commands, as MacFarlane accepts Angus' offering of French brandy.

The revellers sing the first two verses and choruses of "The Bonnets of Bonnie Dundee," Sir Walter Scott's tribute to John Graham, 7th Laird of Claverhouse, 1st Viscount Dundee, who led the first Jacobite rising and was killed at the battle of Killiecrankie in 1689. (The tune appropriated by Scott previously had been used for several songs about the city of Dundee, located in the eastern central Lowlands of Scotland. Scott's version was adapted as a military march by several Scottish regiments in the British Army.) As MacFarlane awaits his dram, the bonny boys of Penicuik rhythmically wave their tankards and sing:

> To the Lords of Convention 'twas Clavers who spoke.
> 'Ere the King's crown shall fall there are crowns to be broke;
> So let each Cavalier who loves honour and me,
> Come follow the bonnet of Bonny Dundee.
> *Come fill up my cup, come fill up my can,*
> *Come saddle your horses, and call up your men;*
> *Come open the West Port and let me gae free,*
> *And it's room for the bonnets of Bonny Dundee!*
> Dundee he is mounted, he rides up the street,
> The bells are rung backward, the drums they are beat;
> But the Provost, *douce* man, said, "Just e"en let him be,
> The *Gude* Townis *weel* quit of that De'il Dundee."
> *Come fill up my cup, come fill up my can,*
> *Come saddle your horses, and call up your men;*
> *Come open the West Port and let me gae free,*
> *And it's room for the bonnets of Bonny Dundee!*

At Penicuik, the Fishers Tryst revellers' rendition of Sir Walter Scott's "The Bonnets of Bonnie Dundee" is interrupted by a funeral party.

When Fettes arrives with his encouraging report, MacFarlane crows, "I *knew* it. I knew it—the moment I was rid of him."

"Who?" asks Fettes.

"Gray," states MacFarlane. "I'm rid of him." He then lies to the lad about "induc[ing] him to leave Edinburgh. "He'll bother me no more." Hoisting his dram, he toasts, "Here's to a *good riddance*." Downing the brandy, he vows, "Now that he's gone, I'll be a *new man*, Fettes, and a *better teacher*. The doctors from my school will *perform miracles*."

On the heels of the word "miracles," the pub door opens and in steps a mourning party of four. As the singers complete the second chorus of "Bonnie Dundee," the barmaid curtails their carousal, informing them, "The McCreadys are here. They've come from burying their sister in Glencorse Kirkyard."

Silence reigns, but MacFarlane tells Fettes, "Glencorse—that's a lonely cemetery. Not a soul around for miles."

"Those people will be thinking of that," notes Fettes.

MacFarlane's self-interest has never been bolder: "I'm not thinking about *them*. It's our own ends I'm thinking about."

But this tune sounds too familiar to Fettes. "You've no thought of *going there*?"

MacFarlane, truly ready to get down to earth, admits, "Gray's not the only man who can handle a mattock and shovel. I've had some practice in the art."

"You *couldn't do that*, Doctor," Fettes insists.

"I let no opportunity escape me," he argues. "I've a whole new course of lectures for you fellows. We'll *need* subjects to demonstrate. Come on!" he commands as he rises to leave, but Fettes refuses. "Why not?" asks MacFarlane. "I *must* have subjects. It's the only way I can teach. It's the only way you can learn. The stupidity of the people, the idiocy of their laws, shall not stop me. Nor will they force me to deal with reptilian creatures like Gray! We can do our own dirty work—and we will. Let's go!"

Fettes (Russell Wade) and Dr. MacFarlane (Henry Daniell) at the Fishers Tryst.

In this scene, Fettes joins MacFarlane, not to rob graves, but only to inform him of the successful surgery. In Stevenson's story, Dr. K--- orders both men to rifle the grave at Glencorse. (The very idea of Georgina's spinal problems may have been inspired by an aspect of the June 1828 double murder, during which the deaf-mute boy reportedly had his spine snapped by Burke before his corpse was delivered, with that of his grandmother, to Dr. Knox in a herring barrel.)

In the story, while sharing, not just a drink, but a full meal with Macfarlane at the Fishers Tryst, Stevenson's "lion"-like Fettes boasts openly:

> Late one afternoon the pair set forth, well wrapped in cloaks and furnished with a formidable bottle. It rained without remission—a cold, dense, lashing rain. Now and again there blew a puff of wind, but these sheets of falling water kept it down. Bottle and all, it was a sad and silent drive as far as Penicuik, where they were to spend the evening. They stopped once, to hide their implements in a thick bush not far from the churchyard, and once again at the Fishers Tryst, to have a toast before the kitchen fire and vary their nips of whisky with a glass of ale. When they reached their journey's end the gig was housed, the horse was fed and comforted, and the two young doctors in a private room sat down to the best dinner and the best wine the house afforded. The lights, the fire, the beating rain upon the window, the cold, incongruous work that lay before them, added zest to their enjoyment of the meal. With every glass their cordiality increased. Soon Macfarlane handed a little pile of gold to his companion.
>
> "A compliment," he said. "Between friends these little d---d accommodations ought to fly like pipe-lights."
>
> Fettes pocketed the money, and applauded the sentiment to the echo. "You are a philosopher," he cried. "I was an ass till I knew you. You and K--- between you, by the Lord Harry! but you'll make a man of me."

> "Of course, we shall," applauded Macfarlane. "A man? I tell you, it required a man to back me up the other morning. There are some big, brawling, forty-year-old cowards who would have turned sick at the look of the d---d thing; but not you—you kept your head. I watched you."
>
> "Well, and why not?" Fettes thus vaunted himself.
>
> "It was no affair of mine. There was nothing to gain on the one side but disturbance, and on the other I could count on your gratitude, don't you see?" And he slapped his pocket till the gold pieces rang.
>
> Macfarlane somehow felt a certain touch of alarm at these unpleasant words. He may have regretted that he had taught his young companion so successfully, but he had no time to interfere, for the other noisily continued in this boastful strain:
>
> "The great thing is not to be afraid. Now, between you and me, I don't want to hang—that's practical; but for all cant, Macfarlane, I was born with a contempt. Hell, God, Devil, right, wrong, sin, crime, and all the old gallery of curiosities—they may frighten boys, but men of the world, like you and me, despise them. Here's to the memory of Gray!"

As directed by Robert Wise and Mark Robson, Stevenson's harrowing climax is one of the most frightening four-minute scenes ever filmed, and the first sequence in a horror film to feature Karloff, not as a resurrected corpse, but as a bona fide "dead body." The fact that Lewton used the literary passage as a virtual blueprint for the cinematic sequence (superbly edited by J. R. Whittredge) is lent additional interest by Wise's shooting of many of the coach-interior setups featuring Karloff and Daniell on Stevenson's birthday (which was thoroughly coincidental):

> They were so nearly at an end of their abhorred task that they judged it wisest to complete it in the dark. The coffin was exhumed and broken open; the body inserted in the dripping sack and carried between them to the gig; one

mounted to keep it in its place, and the other, taking the horse by the mouth, groped along by wall and bush until they reached the wider road by the Fishers Tryst. Here was a faint, diffused radiancy, which they hailed like daylight; by that they pushed the horse to a good pace and began to rattle along merrily in the direction of the town.

They had both been wetted to the skin during their operations, and now, as the gig jumped among the deep ruts, the thing that stood propped between them fell now upon one and now upon the other. At every repetition of the horrid contact each instinctively repelled it with the greater haste; and the process, natural although it was, began to tell upon the nerves of the companions. Macfarlane made some ill-favoured jest about the farmer's wife, but it came hollowly from his lips, and was allowed to drop in silence. Still their unnatural burden bumped from side to side; and now the head would be laid, as if in confidence, upon their shoulders, and now the drenching sackcloth would flap icily about their faces. A creeping chill began to possess the soul of Fettes. He peered at the bundle, and it seemed somehow larger than at first. All over the countryside, and from every degree of distance, the farm dogs accompanied their passage with tragic ululations; and it grew and grew upon his mind that some unnatural miracle had been accomplished, that some nameless change had befallen the dead body, and that it was in fear of their unholy burden that the dogs were howling.

"For God's sake," said he, making a great effort to arrive at speech, "for God's sake, let's have a light!"

Seemingly Macfarlane was affected in the same direction; for, though he made no reply, he stopped the horse, passed the reins to his companion, got down, and proceeded to kindle the remaining lamp. They had by that time got no farther than the cross-road down to Auchenclinny. The rain still poured as though the deluge were returning, and it was no easy matter to make a light in such a world of wet and darkness. When at last the flickering blue flame had been transferred to the wick and began to expand and clarify, and shed a wide circle of misty brightness round the gig, it became possible for the two young men to see each other and the thing they had along with them. The rain had moulded the rough sacking to the outlines of the body underneath; the head was distinct from the trunk, the shoulders plainly modelled; something at once spectral and human riveted their eyes upon the ghastly comrade of their drive.

For some time Macfarlane stood motionless, holding up the lamp. A nameless dread was swathed, like a wet sheet, about the body, and tightened the white skin upon the face of Fettes; a fear that was meaningless, a horror of what could not be, kept mounting to his brain. Another beat of the watch, and he had spoken. But his comrade forestalled him.

"That is not a woman," said Macfarlane in a hushed voice.

"It was a woman when we put her in," whispered Fettes.

"Hold that lamp," said the other. "I must see her face."

And as Fettes took the lamp his companion untied the fastenings of the sack and drew down the cover from the head. The light fell very clear upon the dark, well-moulded features and smooth-shaven cheeks of a too familiar countenance, often beheld in dreams of both of these young men. A wild yell rang up into the night; each leaped from his own side into the roadway; the lamp fell, broke and was extinguished; and the horse, terrified by this unusual commotion, bounded and went off toward Edinburgh at a gallop, bearing along with it, sole occupant of the gig, the body of the dead and long-dissected Gray.

In the film, after killing and dissecting Gray, MacFarlane believes he has seen the last of his tormentor; but, as he and Fettes drive back to Edinburgh with the corpse of the old woman they have stolen, the

Halting the coach in pouring rain, Dr. MacFarlane (Henry Daniell) tells Fettes, "'I swear, it's *changed*!"

doctor hears voices. Gray's sepulchral declarations induce MacFarlane to stop the coach, the light from Fettes' lantern falling on the corpse. Here, a shot from MacFarlane's point of view shows the doctor (and the audience) that the corpse *has* changed. MacFarlane's yell spooks the horse into a rapid charge, sending the doctor to his death at the bottom of a gorge. The imagery used during MacFarlane's hallucination is particularly strong, with the emaciated Gray appearing to embrace him as the coach speeds off.

These four minutes contain 64 cuts that utilize 26 camera setups. The shots form a montage not unlike a musical crescendo, increasing dramatically as it progresses. Wise's editing talent is apparent (he cut *Citizen Kane* in 1941), as the tempo of the scene does not draw attention to itself. Shots of the exterior of the gig (as directed by Robson, always photographed in medium long shot) are placed strategically within the scene. The first setup, an establishing shot of the gig on the road, is followed by 10 shots of the characters within the gig. This structure is repeated four times, after which shots of the gig on the road and shots of the characters are alternated, lasting less screen time at each interval. This method of balanced editing, culminating with rapidly cut alternating shots (achieved by the keen timing of Whittredge), creates a very frenzied, uneasy atmosphere.

MacFarlane and Fettes are photographed consistently with the camera placed outside the coach, a technique which adds to the claustrophobic mood of the scene. Prior to the accident, Fettes' point of view is never shown, and the camera is placed to the right of MacFarlane, with the doctor in the foreground and Fettes in the background. Long shots are not included, even when the coach is shown on the road; these images are photographed in medium or medium long shot, helping to maintain the impressive ambience. MacFarlane's point of view is featured only when Gray's face appears, providing the height of the doctor's terror and a dramatic climax; the close of the scene includes the same type of composition from

Fettes (Russell Wade) is ordered by MacFarlane, "Hold that lamp up. I must see her face."

Dr. MacFarlane (Henry Daniell) sees "Gray!"

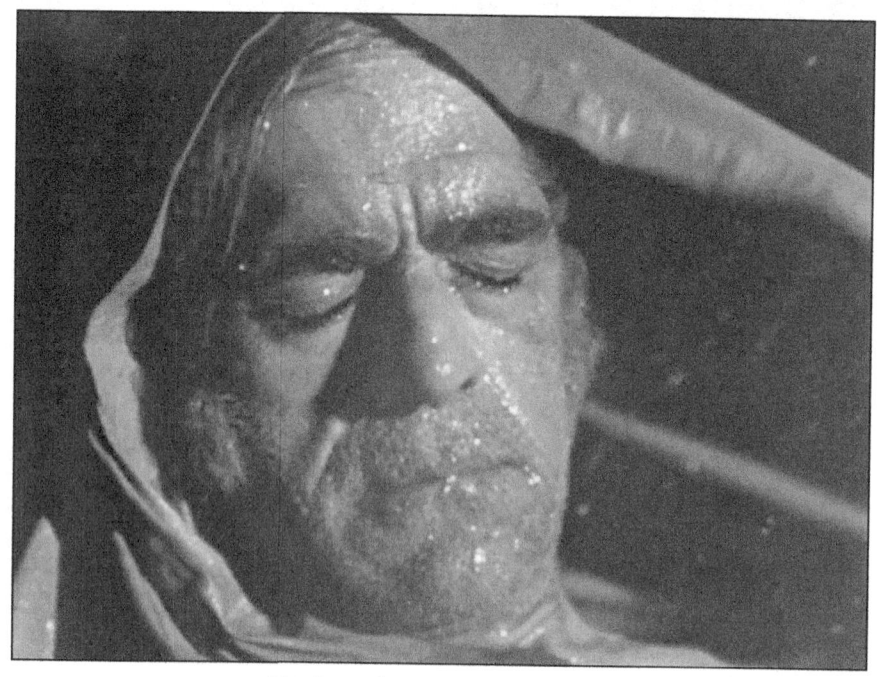

The face of Gray (Boris Karloff)?

Fettes' viewpoint, proving that MacFarlane was slain by his troubled conscience.

In the story, Stevenson has both Macfarlane and Fettes see the face of Gray before they frantically abandon the gig. Unlike the film's resolution of killing the doctor, Stevenson allows him to live, only to be haunted by the memory of Gray's spirit (hence his strong reaction when Fettes asks, "Have you seen it again?") Stevenson presents Fettes as a worn-out, broken drunkard, a primarily unfeeling man who also has been punished by the apparition of Gray. Not only did he follow Macfarlane's orders while working for Dr. K---, but he also chose to become a "lion," even after expressing reservations about accepting the corpses of both the Street Singer and Gray.

A reason for Lewton's decision to modify the very tail-end of the story, in which Fettes reveals the face of the dead woman, is offered by J. P. Telotte:

> Knowing...that grotesque visions, given their initial shock effect, cannot stand sustained scrutiny—by the camera or the human eye—that they tend to become "something to laugh at," Lewton and... Wise altered the final horrific scene... giving it a more hallucinatory effect and joining it to a characteristically archetypal concluding image. In general the adaptation shares the typical structural distinctions of the other works in the [Lewton] series: complex recurring images, atmospheric and metaphoric settings, paired scenes to generate an ironic effect, and the use of characters to link scenes and plot elements... "some unnatural miracle," as Stevenson describes it, transforms the body of a local farmer's wife into that of Gray. With this discovery "a fear that was meaningless, a horror of what could not be" afflicts the graverobbers, and with this single shocking discovery and sudden plunge into the supernatural it implies the narrative simply breaks off. Having transported us fully into this fantastic realm, Stevenson never returns to his narrator's privileged perspective and the frame of his frame-tale. Rather than belabour an

obvious moral, he simply demonstrates how man's desires can lead him into that blindness and trap him within a haunting nightmare world largely of his own creation. The image of Gray stands as a cautionary note for the tale, a reminder of what we might "dig up" once we divorce scientific endeavor from ethical guidance.[11]

Shots of Edinburgh Castle and Holyrood are integrated successfully into the initial scene, and the recreations of the Fishers Tryst and Glencorse cemetery lend an authentic ambience. But perhaps the most impressive geographical element is the location Lewton chose (and Robson filmed) for the climactic sequence, a remarkable approximation of the Pentland Hills. Heather may be glimpsed in the medium long shots featuring the gig, and the final shot, showing Fettes walking up the road toward some rain-drenched braes, is particularly impressive. Telotte concludes,

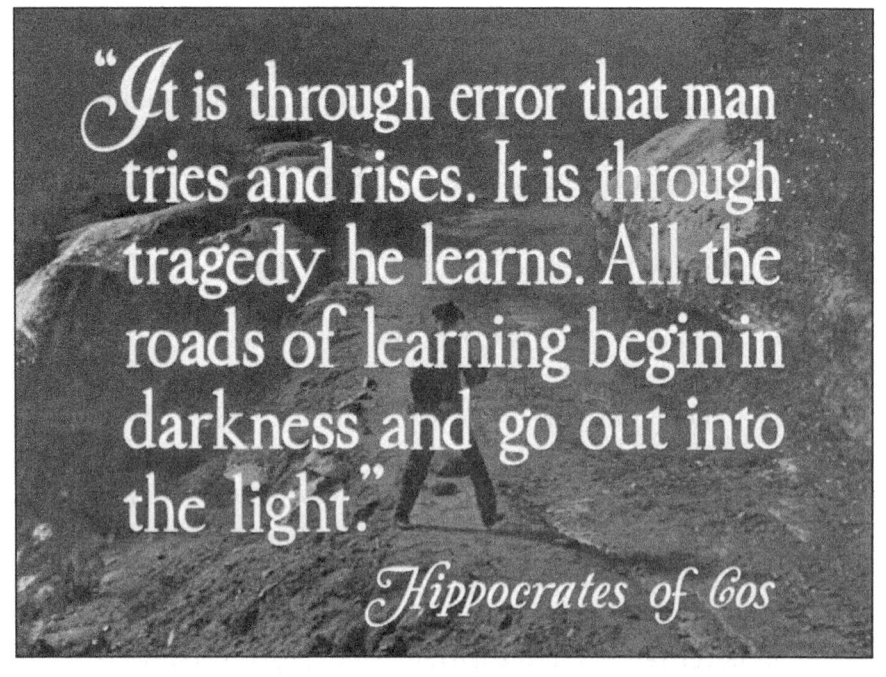

"It is through error that man tries and rises. It is through tragedy he learns. All the roads of learning begin in darkness and go out into the light."
Hippocrates of Cos

Borrowed from Hippocrates, the moral of the screen story.

Within this vista, Fettes seems a small, fragile figure, although one who now carries a deeper understanding of both his world and himself....Having survived this encounter, Fettes takes with him a larger knowledge than he could ever have gained from MacFarlane and his scientific expertise, which, like the lamp he carries, might light his way along the hazardous paths he has yet to travel.... *The Body Snatcher* offers a vision of grotesquery more subtle, yet also more truly photogenic than that found among the ghouls and monsters which so populated the horror genre during the 1940s. In focusing our attention beneath the surface, on man and his actions in all their ambiguity of motivation and unintended effect, this film, like its predecessors, revealed those more unsettling horrors that come from within, manifestations of the ghosts with which we commonly haunt our own lives as a result of the deals we try to work with death itself.[12]

Art director Albert S. D'Agostino's approximation of the braes between Penicuik and Edinburgh surround Fettes (Russell Wade) at the beginning of his new journey.

The character of Gray proves that a film adaptation does not have to adhere slavishly to every word of a literary original to do it artistic justice (particularly a short story, which invariably must be expanded for feature-film length). With *The Body Snatcher*, Lewton and company took Stevenson's ideas and made them more clear and interesting to both the reader and film viewer. Stevenson's tendency to create morally ambiguous characters is only sporadically evident in the story.

The literary Macfarlane truly believes that the human race is composed of two distinct types of people: "Why, man, do you know what this life is? There are two squads of us—the lions and the lambs. If you're a lamb, you'll come to lie on these tables like Gray or Jane Galbraith; if you're a lion, you'll live and drive a horse like me, like K---, like all the world with any wit or courage."

Perhaps Stevenson believed that this distinction would link Macfarlane with the racist Robert Knox, or would drive home the effectiveness of the story's ending. But moral complexity is a stronger component in the film version. Arguably, Lewton's *The Body Snatcher* can be viewed as the sole example of a film adaptation being more faithful to Stevenson's general style than the literary work itself. (However, Stevenson wrote "The Body-Snatcher" early in his fictional career, at a time when he was beginning to develop a distinctive style. Obviously, Lewton had access to Stevenson's later works as well.)

Stevenson depicts Macfarlane as a lion, but the cinematic character is less rigid. Rather than expressing himself in Stevenson's terms, he frequently appears angst-ridden and unable to pursue objectives that will bring him personal and public success. At several points, the audience may empathize with him, particularly when viewing Gray's dead face at the end. MacFarlane and Gray often appear to be two parts of one larger entity, with neither of them able to function without the other, a factor reinforced by Henry Daniell's incisive and powerful portrayal, splendidly complementing that of Karloff. Lewton and Daniell made MacFarlane an ultimately tragic character.

The cinematic Gray is a far cry from the "coarse, vulgar and stupid" character described by Stevenson in the story. Not only does he convince MacFarlane to perform the surgery and then provide him with a necessary research subject, his kindness to Georgina ultimately inspires her to walk.

Karloff's fully realized portrayal of Gray occasionally is reminiscent of Stevenson's "Sea Cook," Long John Silver, a literary creation possessing a great range of both "good" and "bad" qualities. Like Silver in *Treasure Island*, Gray performs morally evil actions incited by his environment: To an extent, he cannot help the situation he has fallen into, due to the society in which he was raised, with its rigid class distinctions and poverty. Gray may believe his act of murdering in the line of duty (working to supply "humane" researchers with subjects) may exonerate him from killing the Street Singer.

Throughout the film, Gray and MacFarlane appear to exchange elements of their personalities. While the former contributes to Georgina's cure, the latter becomes a manipulative and self-serving graverobber. When MacFarlane boasts that he is "rid of him forever" and then tells Fettes that he will no longer require the services of "reptilian creatures like Gray," he has become the very thing he is trying to destroy. His ultimate disregard for others is foreshadowed in the earlier scene when Meg tells Fettes that he has forced her to pose as his maid.

Being typecast in the horror genre for 13 years, Karloff seldom had the chance to interpret such a magnificently complicated and literate character. Gray gave him the opportunity to craft one of his most finely textured cinematic performances. He is genuinely frightening but also magnetically attractive to the audience.

Aside from the flawed sequence involving the fight between Gray and MacFarlane, *The Body Snatcher* is consistently impressive during its 78-minute running time. Brilliantly expanded from Stevenson's story by Lewton, who added both depth and breadth to the major characters and plot, as well as incorporating details from the Burke and Hare case and other elements from relevant Scottish history and culture, the carefully crafted, literate screenplay (with contributions from Philip MacDonald) was realized (blending effective macabre and shock moments with taste and restraint) by a uniformly excellent production team, particularly Robert Wise, Robert De Grasse, J. R. Whittredge, Roy Webb, and the art direction team of Albert S. D'Agostino and Walter E. Keller.

Although the entire film was shot in the studio and at the RKO ranch, Lewton and Wise were able to evoke a convincing atmosphere of 1831 Scotland, aided substantially by Webb's musical contributions, which greatly enhance the art direction. Lewton and Webb's use of "Will Ye No Cam Back Again?" which reaches back to the 1745 Rebellion, also links *The Body Snatcher* tangentially to Stevenson's *Kidnapped*, *Catriona* and *The Master of Ballantrae*, which include several passages enhanced with Jacobite-era music.

Though Karloff, after appearing in *The Climax* and *House of Frankenstein* (both 1944), was pleased to be released from Universal's sequel mill, he did not, as Joel Siegel has written, try to "shake off his horrific screen image." Noting that Karloff was "a gentleman of culture" and, therefore, sought to discard his popular persona, Siegel haughtily claimed that Karloff "had never before, especially at Universal, worked with a man of such taste and refinement."[13] Although the actor may not have collaborated with another person possessing Lewton's sheer intellectual prowess, this attitude discounts the considerable cinematic talent of Universal directors James Whale, Karl Freund and Edgar G. Ulmer. Not all Universal films feature, as Mark Robson commented, "a werewolf chasing a girl in a nightgown up a tree."[14]

In *Bela Lugosi and Boris Karloff*, referring to the final on-screen teaming of the two "horror men," Gregory Mank concludes,

> Boris Karloff's Gray, the "crawling graveyard rat," is one of the most magnificent villains in screen history. ...[Henry] Daniell makes a proud, virile, clever, and cold MacFarlane, his "Toddy" striking, sympathetic and thoroughly tragic—an exceptional star performance from an underrated character player...
>
> And, as for Bela Lugosi... his Joseph remains a genuinely effective portrayal, vile, creepy... Bela's pathetically tragic Joseph is one of his best screen performances. His final scene with Karloff is one of the most haunting in the legacies of both stars.[15]

Dissecting *The Body Snatcher* • 197

The Body Snatcher (1945) window card: Boris Karloff featured in a variation of the William Rose artwork created for the one-sheet poster.

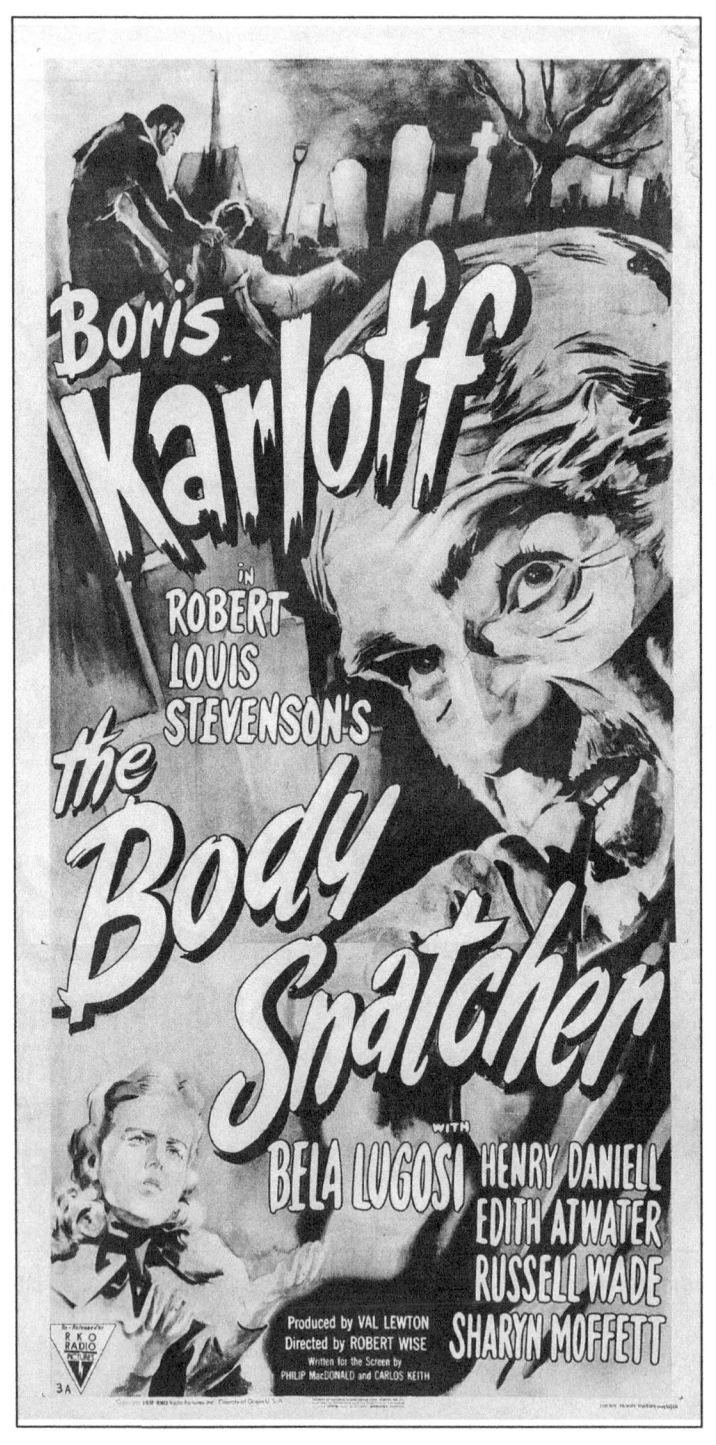

The Body Snatcher (1952 re-release) 3-sheet poster.

6
Resurrecting R.L.S.

ASIDE FROM "THE BODY-SNATCHER," these other Robert Louis Stevenson works have been adapted for the cinema: "The Sire de Maletroit's Door" (1877), "The Suicide Club" (1878), "The Pavilion on the Links (1880), *Treasure Island* (1881), *The Silverado Squatters* (1883), "The Treasure of Franchard" (1883), *The Black Arrow: A Tale of the Two Roses* (1883), *The Strange Case of Dr. Jekyll and Mr. Hyde* (1885), *Kidnapped* (1886), *The Master of Ballantrae* (1889), *The Wrong Box* (1889), *Catriona* (1893), *The Ebb-Tide: A Trio and Quartette* (1893) and *St. Ives: Being the Adventures of a French Prisoner in England* (1896; published posthumously; completed by Arthur Quiller-Couch).

RKO Radio's *The Body Snatcher* is the sole feature film directly adapted from Stevenson's 1881 short story. In 1952, the studio re-released the film, both as the sole attraction and in a double-feature package with Val Lewton's *I Walked with a Zombie*. In 1959, the Missouri Theatre in St. Louis, site of the lavish Valentine's Day 1945 premiere of *The Body Snatcher*, was demolished to make way for a beloved U.S. institution: the parking lot. The theater was not resurrected.

On February 5, 1966, a television adaptation of "The Body-Snatcher," scripted by Robert Muller, was aired on the British anthology series *Mystery and Imagination*, which ran for five seasons (1966-1970) on both sides of the Atlantic. Directed by Toby Robertson, the 50-minute episode starred Ian Holm as MacFarlane, John Moffatt as

The Body Snatcher (1952 re-release) double billed with Val Lewton's *I Walked with a Zombie* (1943) (pressbook advertisement).

Gray, Ian Dewar as Richardson, Anne Ogden as Jane Galbraith, and John Garrie and Dermot Tuohy as a pair of body snatchers.

Several other films have dealt with the Burke and Hare murders, varying wildly in historical accuracy and technical quality. The British television production *The Anatomist*, directed by Dennis Vance from a play by James Bridie, was broadcast as an episode of *ITV Play of the Week* on February 6, 1956, but not seen in the United States until released theatrically in October 1961. Starring Alistair Sim as Dr. Knox, the film also features David Blake Kelly as Burke, Michael Ripper as Hare, and Adrienne Corri as Mary Paterson. Shot primary on three sets, this verbose, often overacted film focuses on Knox, whose use of resurrection men threatens to derail the marriage of his assistant, a young medical student (George Cole).

Another British effort, *The Flesh and the Fiends* (1960), written and directed by John Gilling for Triad Productions, co-stars Peter Cushing as Dr. Knox, George Rose as Burke, and Donald Pleasence as Hare. Set in 1828 Edinburgh, this fact-based version of the events also features Billie Whitelaw as Mary "Patterson" and Melvyn Hayes as "Daft Jamie."

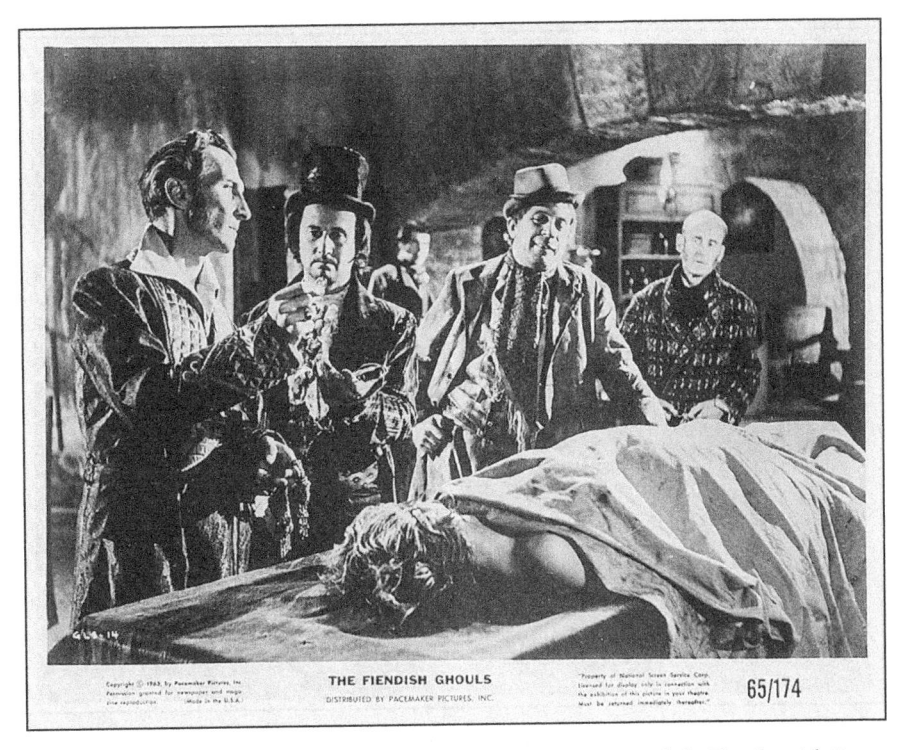

The Flesh and the Fiends (1961), released in 1965 as *The Fiendish Ghouls*, with Peter Cushing (as Dr. Knox), Donald Pleasence (as Hare) and George Rose (as Burke).

(The film also was released under the alternate titles *Mania* [in the United States] and *The Fiendish Ghouls* and *Psycho Killers* [in West Germany].)

Hosted by Boris Karloff, "The Innocent Bystanders" episode of the television series *Thriller*, broadcast by NBC on April 9, 1962, features Victorian body snatchers Jacob Grant (John Anderson) and John Paterson (George Kennedy), closely patterned after Burke and Hare. Directed by John English from a Robert Hardy Andrews script, the teleplay also includes the Knox-like Dr. Marcus Graham (Carl Benton Reid) and Little Jamie (Diki Lerner), based on the real-life James Wilson ["Daft Jamie"].

Burke and Hare (1971), an Armitage-Kenneth Shipman British co-production, was directed by Vernon Sewell at Twickenham Studios in Middlesex. Co-starring Harry Andrews as Dr. Knox, Derren Nesbitt as Burke, and Glynn Edwards as Hare, this Ernie Bradford-scripted

Thriller: **"The Innocent Bystanders"** (April 9, 1962) Hosted by Boris Karloff, with Carl Benton Reid (as Dr. Marcus Graham, top right), John Anderson (as Jacob Grant, bottom left and right) and George Kennedy (as John Paterson, bottom right).

effort also features Dee Shenderey (as Mrs. Burke) and Yootha Joyce (as Mrs. Hare). Released by United Artists in Great Britain, the film was picked up by New World Pictures for U.S. distribution.

Billed as a true story, *The Doctor and the Devils* (1985) was produced by shtick master Mel Brooks and directed by Freddie Francis. Originally written by Dylan Thomas in 1953, the screenplay was revamped by Ronald Harwood and transforms the identity of Knox to "Dr. Thomas Rock" (Timothy Dalton). Set in London, the film is not historically accurate, but features a surprisingly faithful version of the murderous activities of Burke and Hare, and a few elements apparently lifted from "The Body-Snatcher" (including the relationship between Macfarlane and Fettes). The most misleading aspect of the film is its depiction of Dr. Rock as a freethinking humanitarian anatomist who often demonstrates his concern for the downtrodden. The characterization is a far cry from the elitist and racist Dr. Robert Knox, who believed that destitute and "debased" individuals deserved to die.

John Landis directed a "black comedy" version of the now-familiar story in *Burke and Hare* (2010), co-starring Tom Wilkinson as Dr. Knox, Tim Curry as Dr.Monro, Simon Pegg as Burke, and Andy Serkis as Hare. The impressive supporting cast includes Isla Fisher, Christopher Lee, Jenny Agutter and even special-effects artist Ray Harryhausen in a small role.

A quarter-century before he appeared in *The Body Snatcher*, Bela Lugosi played a supporting role in *Der Januskopf* [*The Head of Janus*] (1920), starring Conrad Veidt as Stevenson's dual character in *The Strange Case of Dr. Jekyll and Mr. Hyde*. Directed by F. W. Murnau from a screenplay by Hans Janowitz, the production was German expressionism's entry in Stevenson's depiction of "the war in the members." Before filming began (utilizing three master cinematographers, Karl Freund, Carl Hoffman and Carl Weiss), the intractable Murnau refused to secure copyright clearances and altered the story (an act he soon repeated while transforming Bram Stoker's *Dracula* into *Nosferatu* the following year), drawing his title from the myth of Janus, the two-faced Roman god. Veidt, who had proved a sensation as Cesare, the somnambulist, in the Robert Weine-directed *Das Cabinet des Dr. Caligari* [*The Cabinet of Dr. Caligari*] (1920), was cast as "Dr. Warren and Mr. O'Connor."

The Doctor and the Devils (1985) one-sheet poster, featuring Timothy Dalton and Jonathan Pryce.

Obsessed with his bust of Janus, Warren became the perverted, bestial O'Connor; and, in a Stevenson-inspired sequence, trampled a small girl in the street. Another scene featured O'Connor dragging Warren's fiancée (Margarete Schlegel) into a sleazy brothel. Further quoting the novella, the film ended with Warren poisoning himself. Lugosi played Warren's butler, one of many reasons the status of *Der Januskopf* as a "lost" film is particularly unfortunate. (An original script and a few stills have been located.)

Prior to his role as Gray in *The Body Snatcher*, at various times (during 1931-1934), Universal Pictures considered Boris Karloff for a major role (including casting him with Bela Lugosi on one occasion) in an adaptation of Stevenson's story "The Suicide Club," but the film

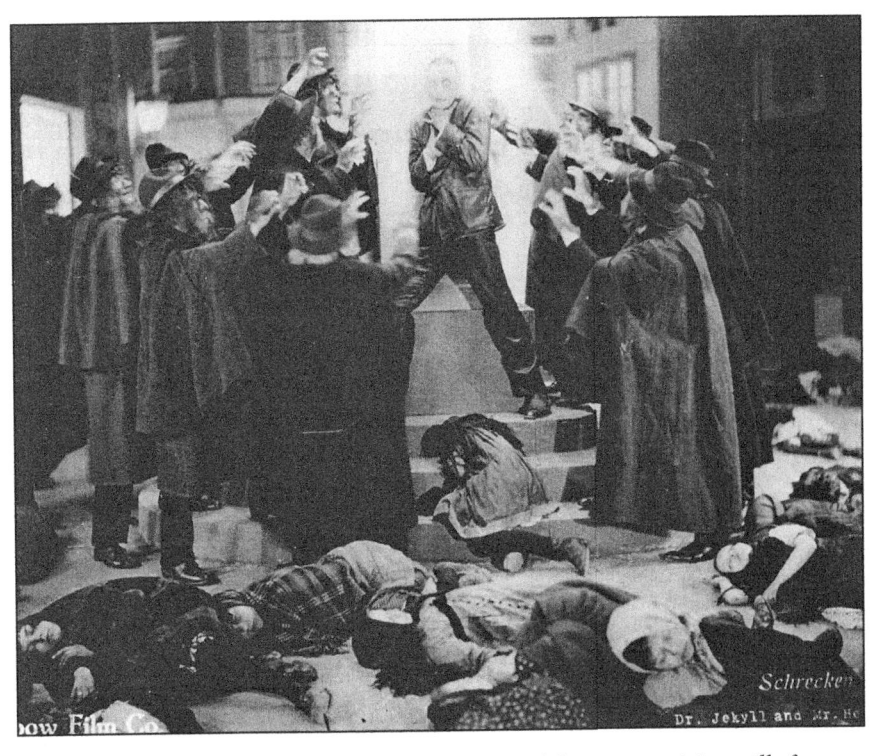

Der Januskopf [*The Head of Janus*] (1920) One of the rare surviving stills from this "lost" German adaptation of Stevenson's *The Strange Case of Dr. Jekyll and Mr. Hyde,* starring Conrad Veidt (as "Dr. Warren") in an expressionistic hallucinatory sequence. (Bela Lugosi plays Warren's butler in the film.)

was not produced. In 1936, Metro-Goldwyn-Mayer released a screen version of the tale, *Trouble for Two*, directed by J. Walter Ruben and co-starring Robert Montgomery and Frank Morgan.

Drawing the dual personality and physical transformation elements from *Dr. Jekyll and Mr. Hyde*, Universal's *Black Friday* (1940), directed by Arthur Lubin, was intended to recreate the popular Karloff and Lugosi combination of the mid-1930s. The screenplay by Curt Siodmak focuses on a research surgeon who transplants the brain of a notorious gangster into the head of a mild-mannered English professor!

Lugosi originally was cast as Ernst Sovac, the surgeon, with Karloff in the Jekyll-and-Hyde role of Professor Kingsley (similar to the parts they had played in Universal's *The Raven* [1935]). However, Lubin,

Black Friday (1940) title lobby card: Boris Karloff and Bela Lugosi in Universal's gangster-horror thriller borrowing from Stevenson's *The Strange Case of Dr. Jekyll and Mr. Hyde*.

The Strange Door (1951) half sheet poster: Boris Karloff and Charles Laughton in the Universal adaptation of Stevenson's short story "The Sire de Maletroit's Door."

who replaced Rowland V. Lee, recast the characters, presumably after Karloff expressed doubts that he could play professor-cum-gangster Red Cannon. Assigning the Kingsley-Cannon role to versatile British character actor Stanley Ridges, Lubin gave Karloff the Sovac role, and Lugosi was reduced to playing Eric Marnay, a gangster who orders a hit on Cannon. Incredibly, Karloff and Lugosi do not act in any scenes together. *Black Friday* marked the sixth of their collective efforts, which culminated with their eighth (fatal) encounter in *The Body Snatcher*.

Following *The Body Snatcher*, Karloff did play conspicuous roles in several more adaptations and variations of Stevenson stories. He is Voltan, a shuffling henchman, supporting Charles Laughton's Alain, Sire de Maletroit, in Universal International's *The Strange Door* (1951), for which screenwriter Jerry Sackheim mixed references from "The Sire de Maletroit's Door" with a host of timeworn horror clichés.

In 1953, Karloff, for the second time, squared off against Universal's inimitable comic duo, Bud and Lou, in *Abbott and Costello Meet Dr. Jekyll and Mr. Hyde*. Arguably an improvement on the previous *Abbott and Costello Meet the Killer, Boris Karloff* (1949), the film offered him an opportunity to build a semblance of characterization. By that time, he had played nearly every horror part imaginable, and now (after Basil Rathbone turned it down) was able to add Stevenson's Jekyll and Hyde to his rogues' gallery. Surrounded by respectable period detail, Karloff played his scenes with conviction, presenting Jekyll as a man who already possesses some of Hyde's iniquitous traits.

Again drawing on elements in *Dr. Jekyll and Mr. Hyde*, Karloff portrays James Rankin, a social reformer in 1880 London, who decides to reopen a 20-year-old murder case, in the British thriller *The Grip of the Strangler* (1957), released as *The Haunted Strangler* in the United

Abbott and Costello Meet Dr. Jekyll and Mr. Hyde (1953) title lobby card: Boris Karloff (as Stevenson's dual character) with Helen Westcott, Bud Abbott and Lou Costello.

States. Theorizing that Edward Stiles, the "Haymarket Strangler," was executed because he could not afford a proper defense, Rankin sets out to discover the real killer, who, in the end, proves to be himself. Much to Boris' delight, director Robert Day, following in Val Lewton's footsteps, chose to depict a strong, atmospheric portrait of Victorian attitudes toward poverty, mental illness and crime, while delivering several well-timed jolts to the audience.

Without using heavy makeup or prosthetic appliances, Karloff grotesquely twisted his face and contorted his limbs (à la John Barrymore in Paramount's 1920 *Dr. Jekyll and Mr. Hyde*) to create one of the most hellish, hideous creatures of his career, providing a stark contrast between the gentle, crusading Rankin and the homicidally maniacal "Dr. Tenant," a repressed identity that resurfaces each time he grasps the scalpel used in the original Haymarket murders.

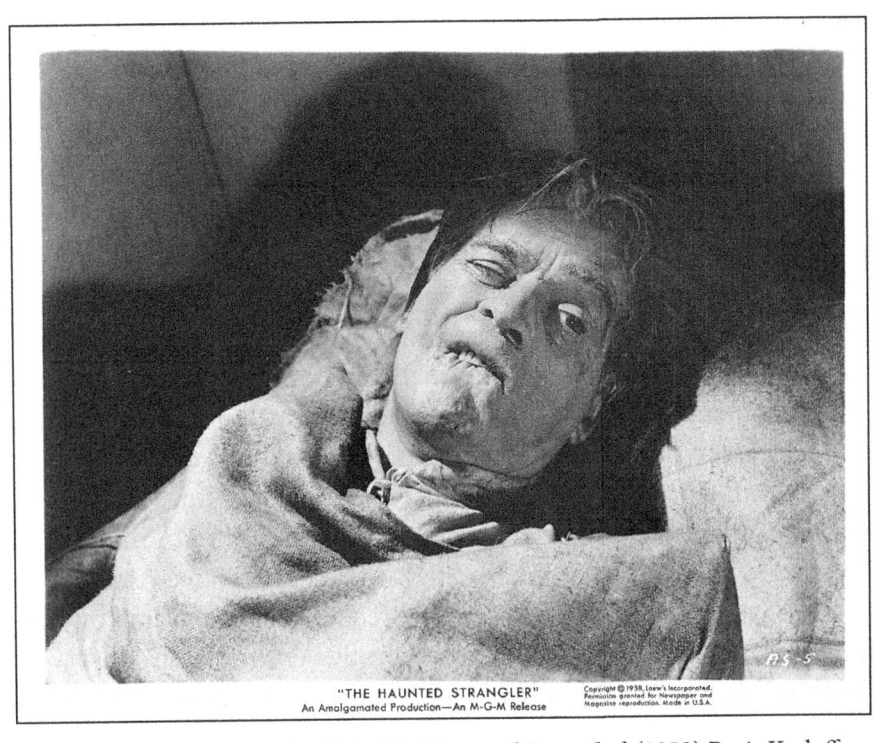

The Grip of the Strangler [U.S.: *The Haunted Strangler*] (1958) Boris Karloff in the dual-personality role of Professor James Rankin.

A follow-up to *Strangler, The Doctor from Seven Dials* (1958) was released in the United States as *Corridors of Blood* in 1963. Another Lewton-influenced Robert Day production, this stylish and atmospheric drama set in 1840 features Karloff as Thomas Bolton, a physician who attempts to create an anesthetic for use during surgical operations. Scorned by other members of the hospital committee, he returns to his clinic in Seven Dials, where he provides free medical treatment to the poor. Unfortunately, Bolton's charity work leads to his association with a local Burke and Hare, Black Ben (Francis de Wolff) and Resurrection Joe (Christopher Lee), who blackmail him into signing fabricated death certificates for people they have murdered in a seedy tavern. Combined with an addiction to the chemicals he has inhaled during his experiments, Bolton's relationship with the murderers results in his own death, but also in his son's successful demonstration of his anesthetic.

On television, Karloff portrayed a thunderous Billy Bones in a *Du Pont Show of the Month* broadcast of *Treasure Island* on March 5, 1960. Written by Michael Dyne, this 90-minute abridgment of the beloved novel was produced by David Susskind for CBS. Karloff played the flamboyant role for all it was worth, drinking rum and singing to the patrons of the Admiral Benbow Inn, where the old pirate captain meets his untimely end. The show marked his fourth appearance in a direct adaptation of a Stevenson story.

The spirit of Robert Louis Stevenson echoes down the ages. The history of the cinema includes precious few faithful adaptations of his literary works, with *The Body Snatcher* being one of the finest, but his overall influence is perhaps immeasurable. Any film featuring pirate lore or characters with dual personalities owes a direct debt to him.

He influenced and was admired by a long line of literary heavyweights, including Henry James, Joseph Conrad, Sir Arthur Conan Doyle, Rudyard Kipling, Sir J. M. Barrie, Marcel Proust, G. K. Chesterton, Jack London, Bertolt Brecht, Vladimir Nabokov and Jorge Luis Borges. In his 1888 essay on Stevenson, James observes, "Each of his books is an independent effort—a window opened to a different view."[1] That same year, Barrie, then a journalist and aspiring novelist, wrote, "Of living authors none perhaps bewitches the reader more than Mr. Stevenson, who plays on words as if they were a musical

The Doctor from Seven Dials (1958) [U.S.: ***Corridors of Blood*** (1963)] Adrienne Corri (as Rachel), Christopher Lee (as Resurrection Joe), Boris Karloff (as Dr. Thomas Bolton) and Francis de Wolff (as Black Ben).

instrument. To follow the music is less difficult than to place the musician."[2]

Stevenson consistently experimented with style, structure, setting and characterization, and he used his versatility to explore several basic themes. Influenced by the tales of historical and religious strife he had heard during his youth, he was fascinated by human conflict: simultaneously the struggle between rival social and political factions, individuals, and the opposing forces operating within the human psyche. His serious illnesses reinforced his understanding of perseverance, a concept first instilled in him by his Calvinist parents and nurse.

His interest in evil began during childhood, and his literary works, from the time of "The Body-Snatcher" onward, illustrate an evolution in his ability to depict the complexity of human behavior and interaction.

His major characters are neither good nor evil; while each may lean toward one of these moral extremes, all exhibit degrees of both. The abilities of a primarily "evil" person are often as appealing as those of a "heroic" one, and his blurring of moral boundaries maintains dramatic tension until the very end, when the struggle either is resolved or, in some cases, continues. He is careful to stress that solutions to major problems are costly and tenuous at best. In his 1887 essay on a novel by Alexandre Dumas, he writes, "There is no quite good book without a good morality; but the world is wide, and so are morals."[3]

Stevenson's status as an amateur musician (playing piano, pennywhistle and flageolet) impacted his professional output, as he often set his own poems to traditional or classical melodies (the most famous being "Sing me a Song of a Lad That is Gone" paired with the tune of "The Skye Boat Song"). He also composed music, and manuscripts of his efforts between 1886 and 1892 have been compiled and documented.

Since Stevenson's passing in 1894, many composers, musicians and singers have adapted his poetry for songs and longer works, including instrumental pieces. In 2009, Sting [Gordon Sumner] set the poem "Christmas at Sea" to music he wrote with Scottish singer and harpist Mary Macmaster.

Stevenson's unique incorporation of historical lore with a modern sensibility often can be heard in the songs of Scottish-born singer-songwriter Mark Knopfler, a Glaswegian raised in Geordie Land, whose vast repertoire includes an array of voyages through his native heath. Stevenson's enduringly popular literature is also some of most globally translated, but his penny-whistle renditions of traditional Scots tunes in long ago, far-off Samoa can only be imagined. Knopfler's widespread works combine evocative, often Scots-influenced poetry with an equally effective, accessible "second voice," the human-like tone he produces from a fretboard. Songs such as "Madame Geneva's," "Border Reiver," "So Far from the Clyde" and "Privateering" are only a few that are evocative of Stevenson: Most suggestive of the author's early Scottish period is Knopfler's 2000 song "What It Is." The lyrical mentions of "frost on the graves and the monuments," "the castle and the keep" and "ghosts and the ancient stones" make it a distant descendant of Stevenson's "Edinburgh: Picturesque Notes" and even portions of "The Body-Snatcher."

Here in the South Seas, today, this "exiled" author and his native collaborator frequently read a Stevenson story, listen to those songs, and watch *The Body Snatcher* in the same evening, while thunder rolls and tropical rain lashes the ramparts. Just now, Stevenson's words, from "Into the Pentland Hills," at the conclusion of "Edinburgh," are particularly appropriate:

> [E]very place is a centre to the earth, whence highways radiate or ships set sail for foreign ports; the limit of a parish is not more imaginary than the frontier of an empire; and as a man sitting at home in his cabinet and swiftly writing books, so a city sends abroad an influence and a portrait of herself. There is no Edinburgh emigrant, far or near, from China to Peru, but he or she carries some lively pictures of the mind, some sunset behind the Castle cliffs, some snow scene, some maze of city lamps, indelible in the memory and delightful to study in the intervals of toil.

As Cabman John Gray informs Dr. "Toddy" MacFarlane in *The Body Snatcher*, "I've never had it explained by so *learned* a man."

Notes

Preface

1. Lachlan Munro, *The Scenery of Dreams: The True Story of Robert Louis Stevenson's "Kidnapped"* (Turriff, Aberdeenshire: Ayton Publishing, Ltd., 2018), pp. 39-40.

Chapter 1

1. Tim Marshall, *Murdering to Dissect: Grave-robbing, Frankenstein and the Anatomy Literature* (Manchester: Manchester University Press, 1995), p. 4.
2. William Roughead, *Burke and Hare* (Edinburgh: William Hodge and Company, 1921), p. 19.
3. Roughead, p. 20.
4. Alexander Leighton, *The Court of Cacus, or the Story of Burke and Hare* (London: Houlson and Wright, 1861), pp. 198-200.
5. Jenny Ward, *Crimebusting: breakthroughs in forensic science* (London: Blandford, 1998), p. 15.
6. Brian Bailey, *Burke and Hare: The Year of the Ghouls* (Edinburgh: Mainstream Publishing, 2002), pp. 77-78.
7. Alanna Knight, *Burke and Hare* (London: The National Archives, 2007), p. 69.

8. Bailey, pp. 78-79.
9. Ward, p. 17.
10. Lisa Rosner, *The Anatomy Murders* (Philadelphia: University of Pennsylvania Press, 2010), p. 225; Owen Dudley Edwards, *Burke and Hare*. Edinburgh: Birlinn, 2014), pp. 175-176.
11. Bailey, p. 95.
12. Knight, p. 82; Bailey, pp. 100-101.
13. Roughead, pp. 157-158.
14. D. R. Johnson, *Introductory Anatomy* (Leeds: Faculty of Biological Sciences, Leeds University, 2006).
15. Johnson; Ross Harrison, *Bentham: The Arguments of the Philosophers* (London: Routledge, 1983), p. 6.
16. Mary Cosh, *Edinburgh: The Golden Age* (Edinburgh: John Donald Publishers, 2003), p. 817.
17. Owen Dudley Edwards, *Burke and Hare* (Edinburgh: Polygon, 1980), pp. 135-136.
18. Reginald Horsman, *Race and Manifest Destiny: The Origins of American Racial Anglo-Saxonism* (Cambridge, Massachusetts: Harvard University Press, 1981), p. 73.
19. Edwards (1980), p. 135.

Chapter 2

1. David Daiches, *Robert Louis Stevenson and His World* (London: Thames and Hudson, 1973), p. 5.
2. Jenni Calder, *Robert Louis Stevenson: A Life Study*. New York: Oxford University Press, 1980), p. 12.
3. David Daiches, *Robert Louis Stevenson* (New York: James Laughlin, 1947), p. 21.
4. Moray McLaren, *Stevenson and Edinburgh: A Centenary Study* (London: Chapman and Hall, 1950), p. 79.
5. Calder, p. 16.
6. Daiches, *Robert Louis Stevenson*, p. 27.
7. James Pope Hennesy, *Robert Louis Stevenson* (London: Jonathan Cape, 1974), p. 128.
8. Hennesy, p. 138.

9. Munro, p. 36.
10. Calder, p. 171.
11. Robert G. Carlsen, "A Word to the Reader," *Dr. Jekyll and Mr. Hyde and Other Stories* (New York: Scholastic Magazines, 1963).
12. Robert Louis Stevenson, "My First Book," in *The Essays of Robert Louis Stevenson*. London: MacDonald, 1950), p. 453.
13. Robert Louis Stevenson, letter to Sidney Colvin, July 1884.
14. Hennesy, p. 160.
15. Hennesy, p. 160.
16. Daiches, *Robert Louis Stevenson and His World*, p. 7.
17. Lloyd Osbourne, "Stevenson at Thirty-Seven," in Robert Louis Stevenson, *Strange Case of Dr. Jekyll and Mr. Hyde, Fables—Other Stories* (New York: Charles Scribner's Sons, 1925, pp. x-xi.
18. Harry M. Geduld, *The Definitive Dr. Jekyll and Mr. Hyde Companion* (New York: Garland, 1983), p. 8.
19. Calder, p. 224.
20. Munro, p. 47.
21. Richard Aldington, *Portrait of a Rebel: The Life and Work of Robert Louis Stevenson* (London: Evans Brothers, 1957), p. 212.
22. Robert Louis Stevenson, letter to Sidney Colvin, 23 August 1893.

Chapter 3

1. Thomas Schatz, *The Genius of the System: Hollywood Filmmaking in the Studio Era* (New York: Pantheon, 1988), p. 180.
2. Rudy Behlmer, *Memo from David O. Selznick* (New York, Viking Press, 1972), pp. 326-327.
3. Gregory William Mank, *Bela Lugosi and Boris Karloff: The Expanded Story of a Haunting Collaboration* (Jefferson, North Carolina: McFarland and Company, 2009), e-book.
4. Cynthia Lindsay, *Dear Boris: The Life of William Henry Pratt, a.k.a. Boris Karloff* (New York: Alfred A. Knopf, 1975), p. 111.
5. Val Lewton, RKO Radio inter-department communication to Jack J. Gross, 10 May 1944.
6. Mank, e-book.
7. *Motion Picture Daily*, 1 August 1944, p. 20.

8. Mank. e-book.
9. Mank, e-book.
10. Val Lewton, letter to Ben Piazza, 11 September 1944.
11. Mank, e-book.
12. Mank, e-book.
13. Robert Louis Stevenson, letter to Sidney Colvin, 31 January 1892.
14. Robert Wise, interview by Van Ness Films. Los Angeles, California, 4 January 1995.
15. *Motion Picture Daily*, 25 October 1944, p, 6.
16. Mank, e-book.
17. Mank, e-book.
18. Wise interview by Van Ness Films.
19. Mank, e-book.
20. Wise interview by Van Ness Films.
21. Mank, e-book.
22. Mank, e-book.
23. Mank, e-book.
24. Mank, e-book.
25. Wise interview by Van Ness Films.
26. Mank, e-book.
27. Mank, e-book.

Chapter 4

1. *Box Office*, 3 March 1945, p. 12.
2. *The Film Daily*, 27 February 1945, p. 2; *Showmen's Trade Review*, 24 March 1945.
3. *Motion Picture Herald*, 24 February 1945, p. 72
4. *Variety*, 21 February 1945, p. 20.
5. *Variety*, 21 February 1945, p. 13.
6. *Variety*, 7 March 1945, p. 12.
7. *Motion Picture Daily*, 16 February 1945, p. 6.
8. *Showmen's Trade Review*, 17 February 1945, ps. 19, 35.
9. *The Film Daily*, 20 February 1945, p. 8.
10. *Box Office*, 24 February 1945, p. 38.
11. *Box Office*, 24 February 1945, p. 57.

12. *TheHollywood Reporter*, 24 February 1945, p. 32.
13. *Box Office*, 10 March 1945, p. 4.
14. Russell Wade, letter to Mr. Mank, RKO Studio, Hollywood, California, 16 May 1945.
15. *The Film Daily*, 2 May 1945, p. 7.
16. *Motion Picture Herald*, 23 June 1945, p. 40.
17. *Motion Picture Herald*, 30 June 1945, p. 11.
18. *Variety*, 13 June 1945, p. 21.
19. *New York PM Reviews*, 25 May 1945.
20. *Photoplay*, May 1945, p. 11.
21. *New Movies: The National Board of Review Magazine*, May 1945, p. 21.
22. *New Movies: The National Board of Review Magazine*, June 1945, p. 7.
23. *Variety*, 13 June 1945, p. 21.
24. *Variety*, 13 June 1945, ps. 21, 28.
25. *Motion Picture Herald*, 16 June 1945, p. 8.
26. *The Film Daily*, 20 June 1945, p. 4.
27. *Box Office*, 27 June 1945, p. 9.
28. *Motion Picture Herald*, 30 June 1945, p. 49.
29. *Variety*, 8 August 1945, p. 10.
30. *Variety*, 22 August 1945, p. 16.
31. *Variety*, 19 September 1945, p. 17.
32. *The Exhibitor*, 26 September 1945, p. 17.
33. *Motion Picture Herald*, 6 October 1945, p. 56.
34. Paul Rotha, *The Film Till Now: A Survey of World Cinema*, With an additional section by Richard Griffith (New York: Twayne Publishers, 1949), p. 508.
35. Anna Lee, letter to Scott Allen Nollen, 3 August 1989.

Chapter 5

1. Daiches, *Robert Louis Stevenson and His World*, p. 7.
2. J. P. Telotte, *Dreams of Darkness: Fantasy and the Films of Val Lewton* (Urbana, Illinois: University of Illinois Press, 1985), pp. 149-150.

3. Telotte, pp. 150-152.
4. Joel Siegel, *Val Lewton: The Reality of Terror* (New York: Viking Press, 1973), p. 155.
5. Bernard R. Kantor, Irwin R. Blackner and Ann Kramer, eds., *Directors at Work* (New York: Funk and Wagnalls, 1970), p. 396.
6. Telotte, pp. 154-155.
7. Telotte, p. 156.
8. Lindsay, p. 112.
9. Robert Louis Stevenson, letter to Sidney Colvin, 23 August 1893.
10. Robert Wise, telephone interview by Scott Allen Nollen, May 1996.
11. Telotte, pp. 151-153.
12. Telotte, pp. 166-167.
13. Siegel, p. 72.
14. Siegel, p. 71.
15. Mank, e-book.

Chapter 6

1. Henry James, "Robert Louis Stevenson," *Century Magazine* 35, April 1888, pp. 869-879.
2. Paul Maixner, ed., *Robert Louis Stevenson: The Critical Heritage* (London: Routledge and Kegan Paul, 1981), p. 323.
3. Robert Louis Stevenson, "A Gossip on Dumas's Novels" (Edinburgh: Swanston Edition, 1911-1912), volume 9, p. 29.

Bibliography and Sources

Interviews and Discussions

Lee, Anna. Telephone discussion with Scott Allen Nollen, 12 August 1989.
Wise, Robert. Interview by Van Ness Films. Los Angeles, California, 4 January 1995.
Wise, Robert. Telephone interview by Scott Allen Nollen, May 1996.

Correspondence

Lee, Anna. Letter to Scott Allen Nollen. 3 August 1989.
Lewton, Val. Letter to Ben Piazza, 11 September 1944.
Lewton, Val. RKO Radio inter-department communication to Jack J. Gross, 10 May 1944.
Stevenson, Robert Louis. Letter to Robert Young, Swanston Cottage, Pentland Hills, Midlothian, Scotland, 27 July 1877.
Stevenson, Robert Louis. *Letters and Miscellanies of Robert Louis Stevenson*. Two volumes. Edited by Sidney Colvin. New York: Charles Scribner's Sons, 1918.
Wade, Russell. Letter to Mr. Mank, RKO Studio, Hollywood, California, 16 May 1945.

Essays

James, Henry. "Robert Louis Stevenson," *Century Magazine* 35, April 1888.

Stevenson, Robert Louis. "A Gossip on Dumas's Novels." Edinburgh: Swanston Edition, 1911-1912.

Stevenson, Robert Louis. "My First Book," in *The Essays of Robert Louis Stevenson*. London: MacDonald, 1950.

Periodicals

Box Office, February-June 1945.
The Exhibitor, May-October 1945.
The Film Daily, February-June 1945.
Harrison's Reports, 24 February 1945.
The Hollywood Reporter, 24 February 1945.
The Independent Exhibitors Film Bulletin, November-December 1944.
Motion Picture Daily, February-October 1944.
Motion Picture Herald, February-October 1945.
New Movies: The National Board of Review Magazine. May-June 1945.
New York PM Reviews, 25 May 1945.
Photoplay, May-July 1945.
Showmen's Trade Review, February-October 1945.
Variety, February-June 1945.

Books

Aldington, Richard. *Portrait of a Rebel: The Life and Work of Robert Louis Stevenson.* London: Evans Brothers, 1957.

Bailey, Brian. *Burke and Hare: The Year of the Ghouls.* Edinburgh: Mainstream Publishing, 2002.

Behlmer, Rudy. *Memo from David O. Selznick.* New York, Viking Press, 1972.

Calder, Jenni. *Robert Louis Stevenson: A Life Study.* New York: Oxford University Press, 1980.

Carlsen, Robert G. "A Word to the Reader," *Dr. Jekyll and Mr. Hyde and Other Stories*. New York: Scholastic Magazines, 1963.

Cosh, Mary. *Edinburgh: The Golden Age*. Edinburgh: John Donald Publishers, 2003.

Daiches, David. *Robert Louis Stevenson*. New York: James Laughlin, 1947.

Daiches, David. *Robert Louis Stevenson and His World*. London: Thames and Hudson, 1973.

Edwards, Owen Dudley. *Burke and Hare*. Edinburgh: Polygon, 1980, and Birlinn, 2014.

Geduld, Harry M. *The Definitive Dr. Jekyll and Mr. Hyde Companion*. New York: Garland, 1983.

Harrison, Ross. *Bentham: The Arguments of the Philosophers*. London: Routledge, 1983.

Hennesy, James Pope. *Robert Louis Stevenson*. London: Jonathan Cape, 1974.

Horsman, Reginald. *Race and Manifest Destiny: The Origins of American Racial Anglo-Saxonism*. Cambridge, Massachusetts: Harvard University Press, 1981.

Johnson, D. R. *Introductory Anatomy*. Leeds: Faculty of Biological Sciences, Leeds University, 2006.

Kantor, Bernard R., Irwin R. Blackner and Ann Kramer, eds. *Directors at Work*. New York: Funk and Wagnalls, 1970.

Knight, Alanna. *Burke and Hare*. London: The National Archives, 2007.

Leighton, Alexander. *The Court of Cacus, or the Story of Burke and Hare*. London: Houlson and Wright, 1861.

Lindsay, Cynthia. *Dear Boris: The Life of William Henry Pratt, a.k.a. Boris Karloff*. New York: Alfred A. Knopf, 1975.

Maixner, Paul, ed. *Robert Louis Stevenson: The Critical Heritage*. London: Routledge and Kegan Paul, 1981.

Mank, Gregory William. *Bela Lugosi and Boris Karloff: The Expanded Story of a Haunting Collaboration*. Jefferson, North Carolina: McFarland and Company, 2009.

Marshall, Tim. *Murdering to Dissect: Grave-robbing, Frankenstein and the Anatomy Literature*. Manchester: Manchester University Press, 1995.

McLaren, Moray. *Stevenson and Edinburgh: A Centenary Study*. London: Chapman and Hall, 1950.

Motion Pictures Classified by National Legion of Decency. New York: National Legion of Decency, 1959.

Munro, Lachlan. *The Scenery of Dreams: The True Story of Robert Louis Stevenson's "Kidnapped."* Turriff, Aberdeenshire: Ayton Publishing, Ltd., 2018.

Nollen, Scott Allen. *Boris Karloff: A Critical Account of His Screen, Stage, Radio, Television and Recording Work*. Jefferson, North Carolina: McFarland and Company, Inc., 1991.

Nollen, Scott Allen. *Boris Karloff: A Gentleman's Life*. Baltimore: Midnight Marquee Press, 1999.

Nollen, Scott Allen, with Yuyun Yuningsih Nollen. *Karloff and the East: Asian, Indian, Middle Eastern and Oceanian Characters and Subjects in His Screen Career*. Jefferson, North Carolina: McFarland and Company, Inc., 2021.

Nollen, Scott Allen. *Robert Louis Stevenson: Life, Literature and the Silver Screen*. Jefferson, North Carolina: McFarland and Company, Inc., 1994.

Osbourne, Lloyd. "Stevenson at Thirty-Seven," in Robert Louis Stevenson, *Strange Case of Dr. Jekyll and Mr. Hyde, Fables—Other Stories*. New York: Charles Scribner's Sons, 1925.

Rosner, Lisa. *The Anatomy Murders*. Philadelphia: University of Pennsylvania Press, 2010.

Rotha, Paul. *The Film Till Now: A Survey of World Cinema*. With an additional section by Richard Griffith. New York: Twayne Publishers, 1949.

Roughead, William. *Burke and Hare*. Edinburgh: William Hodge and Company, 1921.

Schatz, Thomas. *The Genius of the System: Hollywood Filmmaking in the Studio Era*. New York: Pantheon, 1988.

Siegel, Joel. *Val Lewton: The Reality of Terror*. New York: Viking Press, 1973.

Telotte, J. P. *Dreams of Darkness: Fantasy and the Films of Val Lewton*. Urbana, Illinois: University of Illinois Press, 1985.

Ward, Jenny. *Crimebusting: Breakthroughs in Forensic Science*. London: Blandford, 1998.

About the Authors

SCOTT ALLEN NOLLEN received his bachelor's (Film and Honors History) and master's (U.S. and European History) degrees from the University of Iowa. For a decade, he served as a historian, archivist and filmmaker with the National Archives and Records Administration. Since 1986, he has written and edited over 40 books on the history of film, literature and music. His 1994 book *Robert Louis Stevenson: Life, Literature and the Silver Screen* and three volumes on the life and career of Boris Karloff provided the impetus for this tome on *The Body Snatcher*. Born in the U.S. and residing on the island of Java, he still considers Scotland his favorite domain, also featured in his books *Sir Arthur Conan Doyle at the Cinema*, *Robin Hood: A Cinematic History* and *Jethro Tull: A History of the Band*. He now collaborates on all projects with his wife, Yuyun Yuningsih Nollen, and is writing the forthcoming BearManor volumes *Sons of Charlie Chan: Keye Luke, Sen Yung, Benson Fong*; *Sherlock Holmes at Universal, 1942-1946* (with Kris Marentette); and *Charlie Red: The Life and Career of Charles Bickford*.

YUYUN YUNINGSIH NOLLEN, a native of Java, began her literary career by collaborating with her husband on *Chester Morris: His Life and Career* (2020) and *Karloff and the East: Asian, Indian, Middle Eastern and Oceanian Characters and Subjects in His Screen Career* (2021). She combines an interest in research with continuing to develop writing skills in English, her third language, while producing fiction in Indonesian. She, too, confesses a fascination with Scotland, particularly its traditional music.

Index

20th Century-Fox Pictures 57

Abbott, Bud **208**
Abbott and Costello Meet Dr. Jekyll and Mr. Hyde (1953 film) **208**
Abbott and Costello Meet the Killer, Boris Karloff (1949 film) 208
Agutter, Jenny 203
Air Force (1943 film) 78
Alexander III (Tsar of Russia) 53
Alice Adams (1935 film) 67
The Amateur Emigrant (book) 27
The Anatomist (1956 television film) 201
Anatomy of a Murder (1959 film) 78
Anderson, John **202**
Andrews, Harry 202
Andrews, Robert Hardy 202
Arsenic and Old Lace (play) 55, 57, 81
Astaire, Fred 67
Atwater, Edith 65, 75, 106, **137**, **148**, **172**, **173**-174, **178**-179, **180**
"Auld Lang Syne" (song) 151

Bakaleinikoff, Constantin 80, 105
Balfour, George 47
Balfour, Lewis (grandfather of RLS) 19
Barrie, J. M. 118, 210
Barrymore, John 209
Baxter, Charles 25, 42
"The Beach of Falesa" (short story) 60
Bedlam (1946 film) 54, 101-104
Bell, John 7

Black, Alexander 13
The Black Arrow: A Tale of the Two Roses (novel) 41, 199
Black Friday (1940 film) 71, **206**-207
The Black Room (1935 film) 123
Böcklin, Arnold 56
"The Body-Snatcher" (short story) ix-x, 1, 29-30, 33-38, 42-43, 46-47, 52, 56, 58, 108, 130-131, 133, 184-187, 191, 194, 199, 203, 211
"The Body Snatcher" (1966 television episode) 199-200
"The Bonnets of Bonnie Dundee" (song) 80, 181-182
Borges, Jorge Luis 210
Boston Blackie Booked on Suspicion (1945 film) 93
"The Bottle Imp" (short story) 46
Boyel, David 12
Bradford, Ernie 202
Brahm, John 57
Brecht, Bertolt 210
Breen, Joseph I. 59-60, 62
Breuer, Joseph 46
Bride of Frankenstein (1935 film) xii, 123
Bridie, James 201
Bright Eyes (1934 film) 78
The Brighton Strangler (1945 film) 93, 97, 99
Brodie, Deacon 44-45
Bronte, Charlotte 65

227

Brooks, Mel 203-204
Brown, Wally 91
Burke, William xi, xiii, 1, 7-18, **13**, 31, 33, 37-38, 58, 62, 81, 125-126, 138, 146, 159, 164-165, 169, 173, 184, 195, 200-203, 210
Burke and Hare (1971 film) 202-203
Burke and Hare (2010 film) 203
Burns, Robert 46, 151
Butler, Archie 72

Camille (1937 film) 64
Carefree (1938 film) 67
Carney, Alan 91
Carradine, John 3
Castle in the Desert (1942 film) 65
Cat People (1942 film) 54-55, 64, 93, 96, 138
Catriona (novel) 38, 49, 196, 199
Chaney, Lon Jr. 3
Chaplin, Charles 64
Charles II (King of England) 21
Chesterton, G. K. 210
A Child's Garden of Verses (book) xiv, 41-42
China Sky (1945 film) 91
Christison, Robert 11, 13-**15**
Citizen Kane (1941 film) 188
Clarke, Robert 65, 106, **124**, 125, **126, 149**
The Climax (1944 film) 196
Cole, George 201
Columbia Pictures 93
Colvin, Sidney 39, 49, 60, 125
Conan Doyle, Arthur 107, 210, 225
Conley, Renié 105, 138
Connell, Richard 92
Conway, Jack 54
Conrad, Joseph 210
Corday, Rita [aka Paula] **64, 65**, 66, 75, 80, 106, **115, 116, 148, 153**
Corri, Adrienne 201, **211**
Costello, Lou **208**
Coulouris, George 64
Crawford, Gwen 66
Cregar, Laird 5, 57
Crime, Inc. (1945 film) 93

Crouse, Russell 57
Cunningham, Alison ["Cummy"] 20-22
Curry, Tim 203
The Curse of the Cat People (1944 film) 55, 65
Cushing, Peter **201**

D'Agostino, Albert S. 130, 193, 195
Dalton, Timothy 203-204
Daniell, Henry 2-3, 5, **64**, 67, 69, 72, 75, 80, 88-90, 94-**97**, **98**, 101, 106, 117, 119, **125**, **126**, **128**, **129**, **133**, **134**, **136**, **137**, **146**, **149**, **150**, **153**, **155**, **157**, **158**, **159**, **171**, **172**, 174, **175**, **176**, 177, **178**, **183**, 185, **188**, **190**, 194, 196
Darwin, Charles 17, 22
Das Cabinet des Dr. Caligari [*The Cabinet of Dr. Caligari*] (1920 film) 203
A Date with the Falcon (1942 film) 67
Day, Robert 209-210
De Grasse, Robert 2, 4, 67, 72, 77, 105, 114, 119, 130, 138, 141, 143, 148, 150, 156, 169, 195
De Veuster, Damien 48
De Wolff, Francis 210-**211**
Deacon Brodie (play) 45
Dekker, Albert 64
Dennis the Menace (television series) 78
Der Januskopf [*The Head of Janus*] (1920 film) 203-**205**
Dewar, Ian 200
Dillinger (1945 film) 93
Dix, Richard 65
Docherty, Mary 10-12, 14
The Doctor and the Devils (1985 film) 203-**204**
The Doctor from Seven Dials (1958) [*Corridors of Blood* (1963)] 210-**211**
Dr. Jekyll and Mr. Hyde (1887 play) 62
Dr. Jekyll and Mr. Hyde (1920 film) 209
Dr. Jekyll and Mr. Hyde (1931 film) 107
Dumas, Alexandre 212

Index • 229

The Ebb-Tide: A Trio and Quartette (novel) 49, 199
"Edinburgh: Picturesque Notes" (essay collection) 30-31, 33, 212
Edwards, Glynn 202
Emery, John 64
English, John 202

"Famous Movie Dogs" (1940 short film) 79
Fesler, Bailey 105, 119
The Firefly (1937 film) 64
Fisher, Isla 203
The Flesh and the Fiends (1960 film) **201**-202
Flynn, Errol 64
Fontaine, Joan 65
Footner, Hulber 57
Francis, Freddie 203
Frankenstein (1931 film) ix
Franklin, Benjamin 27
Freud, Sigmund 46
Freund, Karl 196, 203
Fury (1936 film) 78

A Game of Death (1945 film) 91-92
Garbo, Greta 64
Garrie, John 200
George, Gladys 64
The Ghost Ship (1943 film) 54, 65, 108
Gilling, John 201
Gone with the Wind (novel) 54
Goodsir, John 7
Gordon, Mary 59, 65, 75, 106, **113**, **127**
Graham, John (7th Laird of Claverhouse) ["Bonnie Dundee"] 181
Greyfriars Bobby (novel) 78
Greyfriars Bobby (1961 film) 78
Gross, Jack 55-56, 58-59, 63, 67, 105
Gray, Ann 10
Gray, James 10-11, 38, 158
The Great Dictator (1940 film) 64
The Grip of the Strangler [*The Haunted Strangler*] (1957 film) 208, **209**, 210

Hangover Square (1945 film) 57
Hare, William xi, xiii, 1, 7-18, **14**, 31, 37-38, 57-58, 62, 81, 125-126, 138, 146, 158-159, 164-165, 169, 173, 195, 200-203, 210
Harryhausen, Ray 203
Harwood, Ronald 203
Hayes, Melvin 201
Heartbeat (1946 film) 78
Heim, Wally 91
Henderson, James 41
Henley, W. E. 42, 45
Hepburn, Katharine 64
Hoffman, Carl 203
Hogarth, William 67
Holiday (1938 film) 64
Holm, Ian 199
House of Frankenstein (1944 film) 3, 196
Hughes, Howard 90
"A Humble Remonstrance" (essay) 39, 42
The Hunchback of Notre Dame (1939 film) 4, 77, 81
Huxley, Aldous 65

I Love Lucy (television series) 78
I Walked with a Zombie (1943 film) 54, 199-**200**
In the South Seas (book) 49
An Inland Voyage (book) 25
"The Innocent Bystanders" (1962 television episode) **202**
"Isle of the Dead" (painting) 56
Isle of the Dead (1945 film) 54, 56-57, 81
"The Isle of Voices" (short story) 46

James, Henry xiv, 39, 42, 47, 108, 210
Jane Eyre (1943 film) 65
Janowitz, Hans 203
Jenkin, Fleeming 25, 35
Joyce, Yootha 203

Kalakaua (King of Hawaii) **48**
Karloff, Boris **ii**, ix-x, xii, xvi, 1-5, 55-59, **61**-62, 64, 66-**68**, 69-**73**, **74**, 75-**76**, 77-**79**, 80-81, 83-**84**, 85-**87**,

88-90, 92, **94, 95**, 96, **98**-99, **100-101, 102**-104, **106, 114, 115**, 120, **121, 122, 123, 129, 133, 134**, 138, **140, 141, 142, 143, 144**, 145, **150, 151, 152**, 154, **155**, 156, **157, 158, 159, 161, 162, 164, 165**, 166, **167, 168, 169, 170, 171**, 174, **175, 176, 177**, 178, 185, **190**, 194-196, **197, 198, 202**, 205, **206, 207, 208, 209**, 210, **211**
Keller, Walter E. 105, 130, 195
Kellum, Terry 105,119, 146
Kelly, David Blake 201
Kennedy, George **202**
Kent, Carl 106, 126, **149**
Kent, Ted J. xii
Kidnapped (novel) x, xiv, 27, 38, 44, 47, 49, 196, 199
King Solomon's Mines (1937 film) 58
Kipling, Rudyard 210
Kiss and Tell (1945 film) 93
Knopfler, Mark 212
Knox, Robert xi, 7-13, 17-18, 37-38, 58, 101, 148, 156, 158-159, 164-165, 173, 184, 194, 201-203
Koerner, Charles 54-55, 103
Kramer, Stanley 104

Landis, John 203
Laughton, Charles **207**
Lee, Allan 72
Lee, Anna 102-104
Lee, Christopher 203, 210-**211**
Lee, Donna 4, 65, 75, 81, 106, **111, 128, 139, 143**, 146
Lee, Rowland V. 207
Leonard, Robert Z. 54
The Leopard Man (1943 film) 54, 65, 67
Lerner, Diki 202
Lewton, Val xiii, xv, 1-3. 53-81, 83, 93, 96, 100-101, 103-105, 107-108, 110, 114, 120, 123, 125, 130-131, 136-138, 142-143, 147-148, 151, 164, 169, 175, 191-192, 194-196, 199-200, 209-210

Lieber, Perry 89-90
Lindsay, Howard 57
The Lodger (1944 film) 57
London, Jack 210
Long, Audrey 66
Longman's Magazine 41-42
The Lost Patrol (1934 film) 58
Lubin, Arthur 206-207
Lugosi, Bela xvi, 2-3, 5, 56-57, 59, 62-63, 66-**70**, **71**-73, 86, 88-89, 91, 95-96, 99, 106, 118, **120, 124, 147, 150, 152, 161, 162, 164, 165, 167**, 196, 203, 205, **206**, 207
Lugosi, Lillian 70-71

MacDonald, Jeanette 64
MacDonald, Philip 2, 58-60, 105, 110, 195
MacDougal, Ann 10
MacDougal, Helen 8-10, 12
Macmaster, Mary 212
Madame X (1937 film) 64
Mademoiselle Fifi (1944 film) 55, 64
The Magnificent Rogue (1945 film) 93
Mansfield, Richard 62
Marie Antoinette (1938 film) 64
"Markheim" (short story) xiv, 46
The Master of Ballantrae (novel) 48, 48, 196, 199
Merivale, Philip 64
"The Merry Men" (short story) 30, 46
Mescall, John J. xii
Metro-Goldwyn-Mayer Pictures 54, 206
The Missing Corpse (1945 film) 83
Mitchell, Margaret 54
Moffat, John 199
Moffett, Sharyn 3, 65, 75, **90**, 106, **115, 116, 117, 135, 153, 179**
Monogram Pictures 67
Monro, Alexander 7, 16, 38, 203
Montgomery, Robert 206
Morgan, Frank 206
The Most Dangerous Game (1932 film) 92

Muller, Robert 199
The Mummy (1932 film) ix, 123
Muni, Paul 64
Murder My Sweet (1945 film) 83
Murnau, F. W. 203
Mystery and Imagination (television series) 199

Nabokov, Vladimir 210
National Legion of Decency 93
Napier, Alan 64
Nazimova, Alla 53
Nesbitt, Darren 202
New World Pictures 203
Newbigging, William 11
Nosferatu (1921 film) 203

Ogden, Anne 200
"An Old Song" (short story) 25
Oliphant, Carolina [Lady Nairne] 80, 141
One Body Too Many (1944 film) 67
Osbourne, Lloyd (stepson of RLS) **xv**, 25, 27, 43-44, **48**, **50**

Pal Joey (1957 film) 78
Pall Mall Christmas Extra (magazine) 35, 42-**43**
Paramount Pictures 67, 99, 104, 107, 209
Paterson, David 12, 38, 148
Paterson, Mary 8-9, 11-12, 148, 201
"The Pavilion on the Links" (short story) xii, 199
Pegg, Simon 203
Penn, William 27
Penrod and His Twin Brother (1938 film) 96
Penrod's Double Trouble (1938 film) 96
The Philadelphia Story (1940 film) 64
Piazza, Ben 59
Pine-Thomas Productions 67
Pleasence, Donald **201**
Poe, Edgar Allan 46, 107
Powell, Dick 83
Practically Yours (1944 film) 78

Prince Otto: A Romance (novel) xiv, 41
The Private Lives of Elizabeth and Essex (1939 film) 64
Production Code Administration (PCA) 54, 59
Proust, Marcel 210

Quality Street (1937 film) 67
Quiller-Couch, Arthur S. 199

Rae, William 12
Randolph, Jane 138
Rathbone, Basil 65, 101, 208
The Raven (1935 film) 206
Rebecca (1940 film) 58
Reid, Carl Benton **202**
Republic Pictures 93
"Requiem" (poem) 27-28, 52
Return of the Ape Man (1944 film) 67
Ridges, Stanley 206-207
Ripper, Michael 201
RKO Radio Pictures xvi, 3-4, 53-59, 61-63, 65-67, 69, 74-81, 83, 86, 90-93, 97-99, 101, 103-105, 109-110, 195, 199
Robertson, Toby 199
Robson, Mark 55, 72, 81, 103, 185, 188, 192, 196
Roch, Valentine 48
Rogers, Ginger 67
Rose, William 84, 197
Rose, George **201**
Rotha, Paul 103
Ruben, J. Walter 206

Sackheim, Jerry 207
Schlegel, Margarete 205
Scott, Harry 72, 105
Scott, Walter 8, 14, 47, 80, 181-182
Scott, William A. 28
The Sea Hawk (1940 film) 64
Selznick, David O. 53-55
Serkis, Andy 203
The Seventh Victim (1943 film) 54, 108
Sewell, Vernon 202
Shakespeare, William 42, 120

Shearer, Norma 64
Shenderey, Dee 203
Sherlock Holmes and the Voice of Terror (1942 film) 65
Sherlock Holmes in Washington (1943 film) 65
Silvera, Darrell 105, 140
The Silverado Squatters (book) 28, 41, 199
Sim, Alistair 201
Simpson, Abigail 8
Simpson, Walter 25
"Sing Me a Song of a Lad That is Gone" (poem) v, 212
Siodmak, Curt 206
"The Sire de Maletroit's Door" (short story) 26, 38, 199, 207
"The Skye Boat Song" (song) 212
Spencer, Herbert 22
St. Ives: Being the Adventures of a French Prisoner in England (novel) 49, 199
Stevens, George 67
Stevenson, Alan (uncle of RLS) 42
Stevenson, Bob (cousin of RLS) 23-25
Stevenson, Frances Matilda Van de Grift Osbourne [Fanny] (wife of RLS) x, **xv**, 25, 27-28, 30, 41, 43-44, 47-**48**, 50-52
Stevenson, Margaret Isabella Balfour (mother of RLS) **xv**, 19-21, 47-**48**, 49, 51
Stevenson, Robert (film director) 65
Stevenson, Robert (grandfather of RLS) 19
Stevenson, Robert Louis ix-**xv**, 1, 19-52, **29**, **40**, **45**, **48**, 56, 58, 60, 62, 72, 78, 80, 83, 88-89, 93, 95-96, 100, 104-110, 118, 120, 125, 130-131, 136, 147-148, 184-185, 191, 194-196, 199, 203, 205-208, 210-213
Stevenson, Thomas (father of RLS) 19, 22-24, 30, 39, 47
Sting [Gordon Sumner] 212
Stoker, Bram 203

The Story of Vernon and Irene Castle (1939 film) 67
Strange, Glenn 3
The Strange Case of Dr. Jekyll and Mr. Hyde (novella) ix, xiv, 44, 62, 108, 199, 203, 205-206, 208
The Strange Door (1951 film) **207**
Strong, Austin (step-grandson of RLS) **xv**, 49
Strong, Isobel Osbourne (stepdaughter of RLS) xiv-**xv**, 25, 49-51
Strong, Joe (stepson-in-law of RLS) **xv**, 49
Sturtevant, John 105, 130
"The Suicide Club" (story) 199, 205
Sullivan, Thomas Russell 62
Swing Out, Sister (1945 film) 93

A Tale of Two Cities (1935 film) 54
Tarzan and the Amazons (1945 film) 91
Thomas, Dylan 203
Thoreau, Henry David 27
Those Endearing Young Charms (1945 film) 91
"Thrawn Janet" (short story) 30, 46
Thriller (television series) 101, **202**
"Ticonderoga" (ballad) 47
Toler, Sidney 65
Tourneur, Jacques 53
Treasure Island (novel) ix, 30, 35, 38-39, 195, 199
Treasure Island (1960 television episode) 210
Treasure Island (1990 television film) 107
"The Treasure of Franchard" (short story) 61, 199
Trouble for Two (1936 film) 206
Tulloch, John 28
Tuohy, Dermot 200
Turner, Terry 83, 85-86
Twickenham Studios 202
Two Thoroughbreds (1939 film) 79

Ulmer, Edgar G. 196
United Artists Pictures 91, 203

Universal Pictures 3, 53, 55, 71, 93, 196, 205-206, 208, 225

Vance, Dennis 201
Veidt, Conrad 203, **205**
Vigil in the Night (1940 film) 67
Vivacious Lady (1938 film) 67

Wade, Russell xiii, **65**, 67, **71**-72, 75, 80, 91-**92**, 93, **94**, 95, **97**, 106, **113**, **118**, **119**, 120, **122**, **123**, **124**, **125**, **127**, **129**, **131**, **135**, 138, **139**, **140**, **144**, **145**, **146**, **149**, **153**, 172, **173**, 180, **183**, 189, **193**
"The Waif Woman" (short story) 46
Wallace, William Vincent 80
Warner Bros. Pictures 79
Waters, Ethel 99
We Are Not Alone (1939 film) 64
Webb, Roy 2, 80, 88, 105, 109, 119, 123, 166, 177-178, 195-196
"We'd Better Bide a Wee" (song) 80
Weine, Robert 203
Weir of Hermiston (novel) 49-50
Weiss, Carl 203
Welles, Orson 65

Whale, James xii, 196
"When Ye Gang Awa', Jamie" [aka "The Duke of Athol"] (song) 80, 127-128, 138, 142-143, 145-146
Whitelaw, Billie 201
Whittredge, J. R. 105, 138, 185, 189, 195
Wilkinson, Tom 203
"Will o' the Mill" (short story) 25
"Will Ye No Come Back Again?" [aka "Bonnie Charlie"] (song) 80
Williams, Bill 65, 106, **124**-**125**, **149**
Wilson, James ["Daft Jamie"] 9-12, 16, 201-202
Wise, Robert 1-4, 55, 58, 62-63, 65, 67, 69-70, 72, 75, 77, 80-81, 88, 92, 105, 108, 114, 138, 143, 166, 169, 178, 185, 188, 191, 195
The Wizard of Oz (1939 film) 78
Woman in Green (1945 film) 101
Wray, Ardel 103
The Wrecker (novel) 49
The Wrong Box (novel) 48, 199

Young Folks (magazine) 39, 41

Zombies on Broadway (1945 film) 91, 93

Made in the USA
Middletown, DE
05 December 2023